Simple Red

Simple Red

A Practical Guide to Winemaking

Otto Fox
Stone Step Cellar
Publications, LLC

Printed in the United States of America

Cover Photography: Lieselotte Fox, all rights are reserved.
Text Production: Heath Anderson

Library of Congress Control Number: 2011900306
Library of Congress Cataloging-in-Publication Data
Fox, Otto
    Simple Red: A Practical Guide to
  Winemaking /   Otto Fox
      p. cm.
    Includes index.
    ISBN-13: 978-1456450458 (pbk. :alk. Paper),
    ISBN-10:
    145645045X (pbk : alk. Paper)
        1. Wine and wine making – Amateurs' manuals. I. Title

Dedicated to my
daughters,
Vanessa, Nikki, and Liese

CONTENTS

Tables

Acknowledgments

My thanks and deepest appreciation to:

Nicole Anderson, my editor, for being my mentor and whose support was key to this book being published;

Sue Bryant-Still, my proofreader, for her skill and expertise;

Robin Rutherford, my wine partner, for his enthusiasm and ingenuity;

Rod Walrath, my consultant, for his insight and great sense of humor;

Heath Anderson, my technical guru, for his professionalism and patience; and

Melinda, my wife, for sharing the journey.

Simple Red

A Practical Guide to Winemaking

Introduction

As a home winemaker I have relished in the experiences of the harvest, immersed myself in the never-ending information made available on the subject, and rejoiced in the rewards of producing a stellar wine. Conversely, I've endured the agony and frustration of missteps, resulting in a precious wine turned toxic waste. I've taken these documented experiences and developed this practical, easy to follow guide. The goal is to simplify this somewhat complex process based on lessons learned.

Winemaking is a challenging experience, even intimidating at times, but the efforts are well worth it. It is rich with information and stimulates the senses. In this book you'll discover how weather, soil, and vineyard practices are important to the overall quality of the grape. On the crushing and fermentation spectrum you'll learn the importance of initial stabilization, sugar, acid, yeast strains and nutrients. You'll also discover how cellar practices involving sanitation, racking, acid adjustments, and final stabilization are critical in winemaking.

To better understand the basics of winemaking, I've identi-fied six fundamental components in this guide, which include:

➢ Grape quality, crushing, and basic fermentation techniques
➢ Advanced fermentation, stabilization, measurements, and adjustments
➢ Cellaring practices including cleaning, barrel care, and racking
➢ The basics of blending, bottling, and storage
➢ Quick reference guides and check-off lists
➢ Descriptions and remedies of common wine defects

I encourage you to experience and enjoy the rewards that winemaking can give you. For the home winemaker, this is a practical, easy to follow guide. For the wine lover, this book provides a deeper understanding and appreciation of the process.

"That which we elect to surround ourselves with becomes the museum of our soul and the archive of our experiences."

- Thomas Jefferson

Chapter 1 - Harvest Day and the Crush

Fine Wine Begins in the Vineyard

The difference between an ordinary and an extraordinary wine is in the quality of the grape. It is the single most important element of a fine wine. Grape quality is affected by its environment, including soil conditions, weather, pests, disease, cultivation techniques, pruning methods, and acid and sugar levels at the time of harvest. The combination of these factors shapes the characters of the wine; the French call it *terroir*.

Terroir

Terroir translates to "a sense of place," or the aggregate of the environment that is sensed in the finished wine. Within a certain wine *appellation*, or geographic region, growing conditions dictate the variety of grapes grown (varietals) and their distinctive flavors and complexities achieved for that region. Agricultural sites in appellations share similar weather conditions, soil, and agriculture methods. For example, I live in the California Sierra Foothill Appellation, where vines grow in a moderate climate at an elevation below 3,000 feet. During the growing and maturing seasons, vines are subject to warm days and temperate to cool evenings. In the Shenandoah Valley particularly, the soil contains large amounts of decomposed granite and is fairly poor in nutrients. These conditions force the vine to struggle for its existence, resulting in a full-bodied red wine with rich, jammy features, particularly in Zinfandel, which this region is known for.

Terroir can also be defined to include rudiments that are subjected to human influences, including the type of varietal to plant, use of cultured or non-cultured yeasts indicative of the area, pruning, irrigation, chemical use, and other agricultural techniques. The concept of terroir means that wines from a particular region, cloned from the same "mother" vine, will remain unique and incapable of being reproduced outside an appellation, even if the same wine-making techniques are duplicated since the elements of the terroir are specific to that area.

Ripeness and balance

As fall approaches, farmers begin to assess their crop by randomly selecting individual berries or clusters throughout the vineyard to determine acid levels (tartness) and sugar (sweetness). Within a micro-terroir, grapes will ripen differently depending on their location within the vineyard (slope vs. valley) or position on the vine (shade vs. sun). Random selection gives the farmer a fair indication on how the vineyard would perform in aggregate.

The grape seed is also an indication of maturity. Seeds that are green or light in color and tart to the taste are usually not ripe. Seeds that are brown, crunchy, and somewhat nutty are considered mature.

The balance between ripeness, acid, and sugar are essential for producing a fine wine. Sugar levels determine the alcohol content and body of wine. Acid levels dictate a wine's drinkability and shelf life – typically, wines high in acid tend to be tart and bitter, while wines deficient in acid are flat.

As ripeness nears, more scientific approaches are employed by the farmer or commercial winemaker to decide maturity, including the determination of acid levels based on pH levels or acid titration techniques and sugar levels based on hydrometer readings, which are described in Chapter 3. Once peak ripeness is achieved, the grapes are ready for harvest.

Where to find grapes

Here are a few suggested places to find good quality grapes for the home winemaker:

➢ Become a member of your local nonprofit home wine-making association. Most amateur wine clubs are established and run by people of like interests to promote information and education in the art of this craft. In many cases, club activities are centered on a common or group "crush" with individual members making wine under the tutelage and support of more experienced winemakers. Club officials and assigned members are tasked with identifying viable sources of grapes from local growers.

➢ Visit your local wine and beer fermentation shop. Besides offering grape sources, most stores provide equipment rental for crushing, pressing, and bottling; chemical and sanitation supplies; educational material; and professional advice on winemaking. Many times grapes can be obtained directly from the supplier or purchased from the store. Crush pad services and training programs are often offered by the store to promote winemaking and, of course, profitability.

> Contact your local winegrowers association. The missions of these associations are to provide information and education to members and support research in viticulture applicable to the area, as well as promote the sale of wine grapes to grape buyers and winemakers.

> Contact your local grape grower or backyard enthusiast directly.

The crush

After returning from the harvest, it's time for the *crush*. All leaves and debris are removed and grape clusters are tossed into a crusher/destemmer, which is designed to remove the berries from the stems and to gently release the juices from the grape without crushing the seeds. This is important since grape leaves, stems, and seeds contain tannins that produce a puckery sensation and vegetal (green pepper or green bean) aroma in wine.

Caution! DO NOT PUT YOUR HANDS IN THE CRUSHER!!

Red grapes are directly crushed or transferred to an open *primary fermenter* (food grade container used during fermentation). These containers come in a variety of sizes and can be purchased from any wine or beer fermentation outlet or hardware store.

White grapes are crushed then pressed off into a holding tank, where they are allowed to settle overnight; later the juice will be siphoned or pumped off the sediment or *gross lees* to the primary fermenter using a wine pump or siphon hose. After the crush and before fermentation, you will measure the sugars, check the pH and acid levels (Chapter 3), and document your findings (Appendix 6).

If you are a beginning hobbyist you may consider joining a local winemakers club, where equipment and supplies are made available through club membership and annual dues. In our winemaking group there is an annual *group crush* or *group project,* which is a great way to share equipment and ideas. In a group crush setting, it is easy to compare your measurements with club members, validate your results, and observe the techniques of veteran winemakers.

After crushing, each member will take their juice, or *must*, home to pursue their own winemaking techniques. These techniques may include adding water to reduce sugar and potential alcohol, adjusting acid for taste and mouth feel, or experimenting with specialized yeast strains for a desired effect.

Stabilizing the must

At harvest, natural yeast cells and other pathogens are always present on grapes. If left untreated, these pathogens may cause wild ferments that result in undesired sweetness ("stuck" fermentation) or the production of acetic acid (vinegar). To stabilize the must, an addition of 25 to 50 parts per million (PPM) of sulfur dioxide (SO_2) is needed to kill these pathogens. In winemaking, SO_2 is derived from *potassium metabisulfite* (PMBS), a sulfite that forms sulfur dioxide when combined with grape juice or water.

To achieve the average dosage of 37.5 ppm of SO_2, dissolve 3.1 g of powdered PMBS[1] in 1 cup of water for every 10 gallons of grape must to be treated. Add or *pitch* the dissolved solution in the grape must. Allow 24 hours for the SO_2 to dissipate prior to fermentation before adding cultured yeast to the batch.

Table 1 - Initial SO$_2$ Additions

Formula for SO$_2$ additions: Gals. of must ÷ 10 × 3.1 grams = X grams of SO$_2$
Example: Dosage for ½ ton batch grapes:
➤ Example: 1,000 pounds of grapes = 120 gallons of must (~70 gallons finished wine).
Using the formula above, you will need 37.2 grams of PMBS to stabilize 1,000 lb of grapes or 120 gallons of must
➤ Example: (120 gallons ÷ 10 gallons) × 3.1g PMBS = 37.2 grams for 1,000 lb of grapes.

---

[1] Potassium metabisulfite (PMBS) is available at all beer and wine fermentation outlets in both powder and tablet (Campden) form. Campden tablets release sulfur dioxide when dissolved in water and are added directly to fresh must or juices 24 hours before adding yeast. Each Campden tablet equals approximately 75 ppm of sulfur dioxide (SO_2) per gallon of wine. I recommend measuring PMBS in the powdered form rather than using Campden tablets since it is used in many other aspects of winemaking and should be readily available to the home winemaker at all times. Keep PMBS in a sealed container under dry conditions to ensure a long shelf life.

Chapter 2 - Basic Fermentation

By this time, you have crushed and transferred the grape must into the primary fermenter and added SO_2 to stabilize it. Make sure that the container is no more than two-thirds full to allow for the gaseous expansion that occurs during fermentation. The must is now ready to be adjusted for optimum performance. It is important at this time to keep the must lightly covered to limit fruit fly exposure and to keep the wine as clean as possible. Twenty-four hours after the initial SO_2 addition, cultured yeast is rehydrated and *pitched* or added to the must, and fermentation begins (Chapter 3).

Yeast is a one-celled organism found naturally in many forms or species. Certain yeasts are used in baking and fermenting alcohol (*Saccharomyces cerevisiae*), other forms (i.e., *Candida albicans*) are opportunistic pathogens that cause infection in humans. Fortunately for us, there are many species of isolated or cultured yeasts available in the industry that provides designer-like characteristics and aromas in wine, by specific varietal type.

As fermentation begins, the yeast converts sugar into equal parts of alcohol and carbon dioxide (CO_2). A solid mass of grape skins, bugs, stems, and seeds begin to float to the surface. As CO_2 gas is produced it pushes the mass higher, forming a "cap" that seals the juice underneath.

The cap will need to be broken up and *punched* into the grape juice for several reasons:

> ➢ To allow full exposure to sugars and nutrients captured in the cap as it is submerged in the solution.
> ➢ To introduce essential oxygen to the fermenting must.
> ➢ To keep harmful bacteria or mold from forming on the top of the cap.

Punch the cap two or three times a day during fermentation (approximately one week). For large batches a wine cap punch down tool is available at your local winemaking shop, or for smaller batches (less than 10 gallons) any stainless steel utensil having a flat surface (i.e., a potato masher) can be used.

Remember to check and document the temperature of the must each time you punch. Optimum fermentation temperatures for most yeast strains are anywhere between 60° and 80°F. If the temperature exceeds 90°F at any time, consider adding frozen water bottles or dry ice to cool it. If the must is between 50° and 60°F, move it to a warmer location to encourage active fermentation. The temperature also indicates when the fermentation is peaking (the highest temperature) and when it approaches completion (rapidly declining temperature).

At some point the cap will stop forming. This happens because fermentation is slowing down, creating fewer CO_2 bubbles to push the solids to the surface. The hydrometer should read near or below zero, signaling the next step of extracting juices from the fermented grapes, or *pomace*, called *pressing*.

Simple fermentation facts for red wine:

➤ In red wines, the color from the grape skin is water soluble, so grape skin contact with the juice during fermentation is essential for color extraction.

➤ In red wines, tannins from the grape skins, stems, and seeds are alcohol soluble.

➤ It is possible to produce a white wine (i.e., white Zinfandel) from red grapes by bleeding off a portion of free-run juice just after crushing.

➤ You can produce a blush or rosé wine from crushed red grapes by bleeding off a portion of the juice after a short maceration or soaking period (a French process called *saignée*).

Simple fermentation facts for white wine:

➤ Many white wines are sent directly to the press without destemming or crushing. This process helps in avoiding excessive tannin extraction from the grape seeds or skins.

➤ This process also helps to maintain good juice flow through a matrix of grape clusters rather than compact berries.

➤ Some winemakers opt to crush and macerate (soak) white grapes for several hours before pressing for purposes of extracting flavor and tannins.

➤ This method also helps to increase the pH of the juice, which helps in smoothing out an over-acidic grape.

Stuck fermentation

Sometimes fermentation may get stuck. This occurs when sugars in the solution are no longer converted to alcohol, leaving residual sugar or sweetness behind. This is determined when the specific gravity (SG) or *Brix* is stalled at or above zero on the hydrometer.

A stuck fermentation could be the result of:

> ➤ Extreme temperatures
> ➤ Alcohol levels higher than tolerable for yeast
> ➤ Use of old, non-viable yeast
> ➤ Rehydrating yeast in extreme temperatures
> ➤ Poor nutrient levels in the must
> ➤ Measurable sulfite levels in the must
> ➤ Lack of oxygen during fermentation

These factors are easily preventable by:

> ➤ Regularly monitoring the temperatures of the must
> ➤ Ensuring that the must is adjusted below 25.5° Brix prior to fermentation, or use a yeast with higher alcohol tolerance (i.e., UV43) (refer to Chapter 3)
> ➤ Using yeast that is less than two years old[2]
> ➤ Adding yeast nutrients in accordance with manufacturer's recommendations
> ➤ Adding yeast 24 hours after the must is stabilized with PMBS
> ➤ Punching two to three times per day to promote oxygen exposure

---

[2] Yeast can be stored in the refrigerator for up to one year and still remain viable, which is determined at rehydration. Make sure to place the yeast in a sealed plastic bag before refrigerating.

A stuck fermentation should be avoided at all costs and is much easier to prevent than fix. Following this guide's step-by-step techniques for balancing and feeding the grape must and providing an appropriate temperature environment is all that is required for a healthy ferment.

Restarting a stuck fermentation requires specific actions to introduce food sources for yeast growth, the addition of lysozymes to inhibit bacterial growth, specific yeast cultures with higher alcohol tolerance, and yeast hulls to help reduce toxins. The complete product line and instructions to restart a stuck fermentation can be obtained from the following sources:

> Lallemand – www.lallemandwine.us;
> Scott Laboratories – www.scottlab.com;
> Vinquiry – www.vinquiry.com; or
> Gusmer Enterprises – www.gusmerenterprises.com

Pressing

After successfully completing the primary fermentation and the specialized yeast strain has converted the available sugars in the must to alcohol, it's time to press the pulp. Pressing is necessary to achieve the maximum return on investment, increasing the volume of juice extracted anywhere from 10% to 25%.

The goal is to remove the grape pulp from the fermentation vat, place it in either a rented or borrowed *basket press*, and separate the juice from the pulp. I recommend using a colander to pull out the pulp and leave the free-run juice in the fermenter. The free-run juice can then be pumped or bucketed directly into your final holding container such as a carboy, barrel, or other airtight unit. The pressed juice can either be added to this container or kept separate. Allow a few inches of headspace in the container for expansion during secondary fermentation.

The basket press (pictured in Appendix 5) is typically made available through your local wine club or can be rented or purchased from your local fermentation store or small winery. This device consists of a fixed plate at the bottom, movable plate at the top, and a cylinder made of wood slats around the sides. The grape *pomace*, or pulp, is placed in the cylinder; a wooden plate is placed on top and is forced down by either a ratcheted threaded screw or hydraulics.

Pressing forces the juice to flow freely under the plate. Apply pressure until there is resistance, stop to allow the pomace to drain and compression to relax, and then apply more pressure to extract more juice. If you press too hard, though, excessive tannins are released from the pomace and the wine may become astringent to taste.

Pressing of red versus white

The main difference in pressing red versus white wine is timing. In most cases, red wine is pressed after the primary fermentation, either when the must has gone dry (no detectable sweetness), or when trace Brix levels (measurable sugar) remain with the hope of the wine finishing off in the barrel or carboy. The must of white wine is pressed prior to fermentation, allowing the must to ferment without tannins. With rosé the juice (from red grapes) is pressed off after a short maceration period for the purpose of pulling color from the peels prior to fermentation. Remember, color is water soluble, whereas tannins are alcohol soluble.

Secondary or malolactic fermentation

For red and sometimes white wines, the winemaker may consider secondary or malolactic (ML) fermentation. Malolactic fermentation is initiated by inoculating a specific strain of bacteria that converts the harsher malic acids into a milder lactic acid (also found in milk) creating a smoother finish. Use a freeze-dried culture (i.e., Oenos Viniflora – produced by Flory Bosa), available from any local fermentation store or catalog. Sprinkle the culture over the grape must and punch it in one to two days prior to pressing. Timing of the inoculation is important and should be considered toward the completion of the primary fermentation.

Freeze-dried ML cultures are somewhat pricey (between $18 and $22 per package), so consider using specialized nutrients to aid in the conversion process. These nutrients are inexpensive and contain a variety of organic protein sources, vitamins, and minerals that help condition the wine for a successful ML fermentation. Mix the proper amount of nutrients in water or must based on product specifications and stir into the remaining juice along with the freeze-dried culture.

As secondary fermentation occurs in the carboy or other container, CO_2 continues to be released, which requires a fermentation trap or airlock to be attached (pictured in Appendix 5). This device, when filled with water, allows CO_2 gases to bubble out of the container without letting oxygen or other contaminants in. It can be purchased at any wine equipment supplier.

Malolactic conversion occurs under warmer conditions, similar to the primary fermentation with temperatures ranging in the 70s. The ML process slows when temperatures begin to cool, and will become dormant in cold conditions. Consider placing your carboy or barrel in a warm, dark room until this process is completed, or cover the container with an electric blanket set at the lowest temperature. Try not to exceed 80°F since this could encourage bacterial growth.

Since malolactic conversion is adversely effected by SO_2, make sure that ML conversion is completed before final stabilization of the wine (refer to Chapter 4). Test kits containing chromatography paper, developing solution and various acid standards (i.e., tartaric, malic, and citric) can identify what acids are integrated in the wine and when malic acid is no longer present. Complete instructions are included with each kit.

Simple facts on malolactic (ML) fermentation:

> ➤ ML fermentation converts one gram of malic acid into roughly 0.67 grams of lactic acid and 0.33 grams of CO_2, thereby decreasing acid.
> ➤ ML conversion will likely increase pH by 1 to 2 points (i.e., from 3.4 to 3.6).
> ➤ An oak barrel inoculated with ML bacteria will always have it despite sanitation efforts.
> ➤ SO_2 suppresses the malolactic fermentation process.
> ➤ Young red wines inoculated with ML bacteria develop mellow, full bodied characteristics, while white wines, such as Chardonnay, develop smooth, buttery textures.

Note: If the malolactic fermentation is not completed prior to bottling, it may occur in the bottle without adequate levels of SO_2. Check ML progress using color chromatography paper, or have it professionally tested at your local winery or wine lab.

Cost-saving tip: If you're making more than one batch of red wine this season, it is likely your previous batch is undergoing active malolactic fermentation. Pour off a small portion of this wine containing the culture and use it to inoculate your next batch of red wine, at the appropriate time.

Chapter 3 - Tailor-Made Wine

The techniques described in this chapter are why wine-making is such a dynamic and creative process. Both educated and home-schooled purveyors of the grape must think about what they desire in a wine. What characteristics are they looking for? Is it fruit, berry, plum, full mouth feel, softness, or all of the above? How do you stabilize the freshness and shelf time of the wine? Given these questions, there are various essential and optional methods used to create a tailor-made product.

This chapter identifies the essential components needed during primary fermentation, including sugar adjustments for total alcohol content, pH and acid adjustments, and yeast selection. Other winemaking techniques are described in more detail, including oak and tannin additions, extended maceration, and malolactic fermentation.

Essential Components

Sugar levels (Brix) and total alcohol content

In a natural wine, alcohol is produced through fermentation. This element creates a major role in the body, structure, and taste of the final product.

Alcoholic strength is measured as the percentage of alcohol to the volume of wine in the bottle. The average percentage of alcohol in wine is between 13% and 15%. Wine that exceeds 15% alcohol is a result of fruit having higher sugar levels and runs the risk of an incomplete ferment. If you are making a late harvest or sherry, which are sweeter wines, adjustments may not be required. If however, your goal is to make a table wine with an alcohol level of 13% to 15%, it will be necessary to reduce or dilute the sugar in the must prior to primary fermentation. This is done by adding water to the grape mixture (amelioration)[3].

A hydrometer (pictured in Appendix 5) is used to measure the amount of sugar in grape juice in terms of specific gravity (SG) or °*Brix* and identifies the potential alcohol based on the sugar volume. The device is made of glass having a cylindrical stem and weighted bulb. The hydrometer is allowed to float in the grape solution and SG or °Brix[4] is determined by reading the scale inside the tube at the point the surface of the liquid touches the stem.

Once the °Brix is determined, document your findings and refer to Table 2 – Sugar Reduction for water additions. This chart is a guide only and is based on the optimum sugar target of 24.5° Brix; you can add more or less water depending on desired alcohol levels and wine body.

Example: If you have 1,000 lb of must with a sugar volume measured at 29.5° Brix, you will add approximately 16 gallons of water to achieve a desired reading of 24.5° Brix.

---

[3] Note: If you receive city water that's chlorinated, do not use it to ameliorate the must. Chlorine reacts with wine giving it an oxidized taste. Use purified water instead.

[4] The °Brix is the traditional term used to describe sugar content in wine and therefore will be used in the remainder of this book for consistency purposes.

Table 2 - Sugar Reduction
Simple Water Addition Matrix

Gallons of water added to grape must (based on weight) - Assumes final sugars at approximately 24.5° Brix (+ or −)

°Brix at Harvest	Approx. Alcohol	1,000 Lb	500 Lb	200 Lb	100 Lb
25.0	14.5%	2.0	1.0	0.4	0.2
25.5	14.8%	3.0	1.5	0.6	0.3
26.0	15.1%	5.0	2.5	1.0	0.5
26.5	15.4%	6.0	3.0	1.2	0.6
27.0	15.7%	8.0	4.0	1.6	0.8
27.5	16.0%	9.0	4.5	1.8	0.9
28.0	16.2%	10.0	5.0	2.0	1.0
28.5	16.5%	12.0	6.0	2.4	1.2
29.0	16.8%	14.0	7.0	2.8	1.4
29.5	17.1%	16.0	8.0	3.2	1.6
30.0	17.4%	17.0	8.5	3.4	1.7
30.5	17.7%	18.0	9.0	3.6	1.8
31.0	18.0%	20.0	10.0	4.0	2.0
31.5	18.3%	22.0	11.0	4.4	2.2
32.0	18.6%	23.0	11.5	4.6	2.3

In this case, add approximately five gallons of water to bring the sugar down gradually and punch or stir into the must. After a few hours, measure the Brix again. Most likely it will be lower but still above the desired target of 24.5° Brix. Add 5 more gallons (or less) until you reach the desired sugar content. Always allow a few hours between each addition to allow the water to fully absorb in the solution. If you add too much water there is no going back, so take your time with this step.

There is a concern that adding water will reduce the quality of the wine, but fruit with high Brix is likely found in a dehydrated condition, so in most cases, adding water rehydrates the fruit without reducing the quality.

It is important to note that the addition of water will dilute the <u>acid</u> potency of the must. If the acid levels of the must are within range, then the addition of 22.5 grams of tartaric acid to each gallon of water is recommended in order to *acidulate* your water solution (equaling total acidity of 0.70 g/100 mL), in effect, creating a neutral solution.

Acid and pH adjustments at primary fermentation

From a winemaking viewpoint, not only is the taste impression provided by acids important to balance the other wine components such as flavor, mouth feel, and alcohol, but it also affects the wine's stability during its shelf life.

Acid

Acid is one of the three essential structural components of wine. It's the level of total acid (TA) that determines the freshness, tartness, mouth feel, and shelf time of your product. Too much acid creates a sharp/sour sensation, and too little creates a flabby, lethargic flavor. The proper acid level is also critical for a healthy fermentation.

The mutual effect between fruit (sweetness) and acid (tartness) is usually referred to as the balance or structure of a wine, whereas acid, which is naturally found in grapes, adds to the sharpness and tartness of a wine, including the crisp character of a white wine. Acid balances out the sweetness of the wine and allows the wine to age properly. A solution low in acid is more susceptible to infection and spoilage by microorganisms, resulting in a shortened shelf life. Low acid can also result in dull, flaccid characteristics that soon contribute to off flavors and a lack of balance.

The optimum total acid (TA) level to achieve in red wine is between 0.6 and 0.7 grams per liter (g/L) and for white wine, between 0.65 and 0.75 g/L.

pH

The pH is a measure of acid strength, whereas TA is a measure of the total acid in the grape solution. In general, the higher the pH value, the lower the acidity level; and, the lower the pH value, the higher the acid. Therefore, a wine with a pH value of 3.3 contains more acid than one with a pH value of 3.6.

The pH is easily measured using a pH meter (pictured in Appendix 5). The pH meter can also be used to measure the TA levels in wine as described in Appendix 2 - Quick Reference for Measuring Total Active Acid. Once pH or TA levels are determined, the winemaker can adjust the acidity, using *tartaric acid* during the pre- or post-fermentation periods (Refer to Tables 3 and 4).

The optimum pH targets for finished wines are 3.3-3.6 pH for red wines and 3.0-3.4 pH for whites.

Note: _Always be conservative_ *and adjust your wine with half the recommended dosage, then retest after a couple of weeks. At this point, taste should be considered before making any additional acid adjustments.*

Table 3 - Acid Adjustments Based on pH

Wines with high pH levels are often flat and susceptible to bacterial infection. To reduce the pH, an acid addition can be made using the following simple formula:

(initial pH reading – desired pH) ÷ 0.1 × 0.13= oz/gal of tartaric acid

Example:

> ➢ **Initial pH reading: 3.85**
> ➢ **Less desired pH: 3.50**
> ➢ **= Difference: 0.35**
> ➢ **Calculation: Difference (0.35) ÷ 0.1 × 0.13 = oz/gal (0.46)**
> ➢ **Calculation: oz/gal (0.46) × 60 gal = 27.3 total oz**
> ➢ **Add half: Approximately 14 oz of tartaric acid.**

Table 4 - Acid Adjustments Based on Acid Readings

Acid Additions - 3.9 grams of tartaric acid will raise the acid level in one gallon of wine by 0.1%, if needed. If the acid value of your must is 0.42 g/l and the desired value is within the range for red wines (for example, 0.62), you will need to add 7.8 grams of tartaric acid per gallon of grape solution prior to your fermentation (3.9 grams/gallon × 2).

Acid Reductions - 3.8 grams of *potassium carbonate* will reduce the acid level in one gallon of wine by 0.1%, if needed.

After primary fermentation ends, the secondary or malo-lactic fermentation begins. This process (as discussed in Chapter 2) tends to reduce the acid and increase the pH by 0.1 to 0.2 points. Final acid tests and adjustments should occur after the secondary fermentation to replenish acids lost during this process.

Many times red grapes may contain high acid levels (>0.9 g/L) at harvest. In order to produce well-balanced wines from these grapes, a reduction in acid level may be desired. However, if you plan a malolactic or secondary fermentation of your wines, the acid levels will ultimately drop by up to 0.2 g/L in titratable acid, sometimes well within the desired acid level for wine. Allow the grapes to ferment; there will be plenty of time to make final adjustments.

It may be necessary to adjust the acid levels in the must for different reasons. Maybe your pH is too high and acid too low or perhaps the opposite. In one particular case, I received some Zinfandel grapes that came in with high Brix, high acid, and high pH. Here is how I dealt with it:

➤ First, I adjusted the pH, which was measured at 3.85. My goal was to bring it to 3.50. Using the formula for acid adjustments based on pH readings, I added 14 oz of tartaric acid (see Table 3 above) to 1,000 pounds of must, bringing it to 3.7. This was followed with a 6 oz addition of tartaric acid for a final pH reading of 3.55.

➤ Later I measured the acid at 0.95 (too high); however, sugar levels were at 28° Brix (I wanted < 25°). In order to bring the sugar down I added 10% of unacidulated water.

➤ Adding water to the must did three things: it reduced the acid to 0.75, reduced the sugar to slightly
less than (<) 25° Brix, and left the adjusted pH the
same (3.55).

➤ After fermentation, I inoculated the must with an
ML culture to convert malolactic acid to lactic acid.
This effectively reduced the acid to a more accepta-
ble level of between 0.6 and 0.7.

Yeast selection

Yeast selection is one of the most important decisions in
advanced winemaking. After the first year of gaining basic
winemaking skills you will begin to seek new ways to
customize your product based on your personal wine style
preferences. Plan to visit several online wine and beer
laboratories that offer a myriad of yeast strains, each one
having a certain effect and compatibility for specific grape
varietals. Also, talk with the experienced staff at your local
fermentation supply store to help guide you through the
yeast selection process.

Many laboratories offer catalogs where the yeast strains are
discussed in detail. These catalogs provide easy to read
matrices that match the cultured yeast type to the grape
varietal and the intended characteristics they provide,
including:

➤ Fruit
➤ Spice
➤ Black pepper
➤ High alcohol tolerance
➤ Mid-palate enhancement
➤ Floral
➤ Mineral

> Agreeable tannins
> Tannin intensity

You can select multiple yeast strains to customize your wines. For example, you may select a single cultured yeast for a Zinfandel batch that focuses on spice with a little black pepper, some mid-palate enhancement, and high alcohol tolerance; or you may choose two or three strains of yeast, each providing one or more of the elements you desire. In this case, you would ferment each lot in a separate primary fermentation container.

After selection, you will need to rehydrate the yeast before pitching into the primary fermenter (see Table 5).

Table 5 - Rehydrating Yeast

Simple surefire method to rehydrate yeast:
> Use 20g to 30g of selected yeast for every 26 gallons of must. > Empty the yeast into 2 cups of warm non-chlorinated water (between 95° and 104°F); make sure you are using a sanitized container. > Gently stir and let stand for 15 to 20 minutes. > Gently stir again. > Pull 1 cup of grape juice from the must and add to the yeast solution; let stand another 10 minutes. > Inoculate the grape must with the rehydrated yeast and mix (punch) into the must, making sure there is minimum variation between the temperature of the rehydrated yeast solution and that of the must.

Nutrient additions

As you pitch the rehydrated yeast into the must, add some food during the growth stage to ensure a healthy fermentation. A variety of nutrient products are available to the winemaker, including: Nutriferm, GoFerm, Superfood or DAP (diammonium phosphate). Product specification and application are available online.

In most cases nutrient application is made in three stages:

> - 1/3 applied during the fermentation onset
> - 1/3 applied during the midpoint (determine this using your hydrometer)
> - 1/3 applied two days prior to pressing.

Time-released nutrient products that contain amino acids, ammonia, and other micronutrients are also available. Just toss a few tablets into the must at the beginning of fermentation, based on the manufacturer's recommendations. The food is dispensed throughout the life of the ferment.

Optional Adjustments

Enzymes

Enzymes are often used in white and red wines, but this is not essential. Enzymes break down the grape pulp to increase juice volume and can enhance the wine through extraction of aroma and tannins, color stabilization, and clarification. However, adding too much at fermentation can result in a messy press and possibly result in the development of H_2S (hydrogen sulfide) caused by excessive deteriorating fruit.

There are many enzymes to choose from with product specifications and dosage provided by the manufacturer or distributor (i.e., Lallemand (Lalvin), Novozymes, Scott Labs*)*. For first-time winemakers, using enzymes is completely optional and not recommended.

Oak powder

Adding oak powder (toasted or untoasted) during the primary fermentation enhances the overall wine quality without imparting an oak flavor. This addition helps to reduce vegetal overtones and enhances the flavor, complexity, and mouth feel of the wine. One to two pounds of oak powder are recommended per thousand pounds of grapes or 10 to 20 grams per gallon of must. Application is simple, sprinkle onto the must after crushing and before fermentation.

Simple benefits of oak powder applications:
➢ Reduces vegetal overtones (volatile organosulfur compounds [5])   ➢ Increases fruit intensity   ➢ Improves stability in clarity and color   ➢ Softens harsh characteristics of new wines   ➢ Deepens wine texture

Cold soaking

An important decision to consider for red wines during the pre-fermentation period is whether to cold soak the grapes

---

[5] Organosulfur compounds contribute to vegetal aromas in wine. Sensory descriptors for these compounds include cabbage, rubbery, green vegetable, and "swampy."

beyond the initial SO_2 wait period. Cold soaking, is the extended submersion of fruit in a non-alcoholic setting to improve red wine color and to provide color stability. During the cold soak, monomeric anthocyanins (a relatively light, simple organic molecule that can join in long chains with other molecules to form a more complex molecule or polymer) are extracted, resulting in increased red wine color in the aged wine[6].

Cold soaking is not recommended for home winemakers, especially beginners. Intermediate vintners may cold soak up to 24 hours beyond the SO_2 wait period; any longer and there's a risk of spoilage and oxidation.

Extended maceration

 Extended maceration, or the post-fermentation soak of grape skins allows the wine to develop a more full-bodied, smoother textured character. It would seem that extending the soaking process would increase astringency, causing the mouth to pucker and leave a dry feeling since tannins are extracted from the stems, seeds, and peels by alcohol; however, the opposite occurs. The increase in soak time allows the normally short-chained tannin molecules to form into longer chains, in effect integrating the tannins into the wine. These longer molecular chains would then precipitate to the bottom, giving the wine a softer mouth feel, similar to aging in the bottle.

---

[6] Tannin extraction does not normally occur during this process since skin color extraction is water based, versus tannin extraction, which is mainly alcohol based.

Extended maceration is not recommended for the beginning winemaker unless you have the facilities to control oxidation, volatile acidity (VA) buildup, or bacterial development. The professionals are split on the value of this technique.

Chapter 4 - Cellar Practices

Essential Practices

Cleaning

There are three sides of clean: visual clean, sanitized, and sterilized. Visual clean does not mean that a surface is free of microbial contamination. A surface may look clean but may have millions of microorganisms. Sanitized is the reduction of the microorganism population to a safe level. Sterilized is the elimination of pathogenic microorganisms. Practically speaking, there are no sterile surfaces in winemaking, only sanitized surfaces.

During the initial crush and fermentation stage, strive for clean but not sanitization. The act of fermentation is a cleansing process, where heat and alcohol produced by feeding yeasts kill most pathogens and contaminants carried on the grapes. However, once fermentation is complete, careful steps must be taken to sanitize all equipment, hoses, and buckets that come in contact with the wine.

Table 6 - Five-Step Cleaning Rules

➤ Rinse – thoroughly rinse all items with non-chlorinated water.
➤ Wash – using non-odorized products such as Trisodium Phosphate, Barrel-Kleen, or other non-chlorinated cleaning item; wash hoses, vats, carboys, and winemaking tools of the trade. Allow the solution to remain on hard to reach   areas for

> 10 minutes or longer. Scrub out stains as much as possible.
> ➢ Rinse – clean off any remaining soap residue.
> ➢ Sanitize – using a solution of three tablespoons PMBS to 1 gallon of water, sanitize your equipment. Let stand in the solution for a brief period of time.
> ➢ Rinse thoroughly.

Barrel care and maintenance

Wine stored in a new barrel should be monitored closely. Aging wine in a new barrel for a lengthy period may impart too much toast or vanilla flavors, which could overpower the varietal or fruit flavors of the grape. Once the desired oak character is achieved, rack the wine to a glass, stainless steel, or neutral oak container as soon as possible.

Steps must be taken to *swell* the barrel (old or new) prior to usage. If not, expect to see your precious cargo on the floor. Swelling is the process of adding water to the barrel, allowing the staves to expand, eventually becoming water or wine tight. Refill often during this process in order to swell all staves top to bottom. A good barrel should become watertight within a day.

An acidic environment should be established in the barrel prior to filling with wine. Dissolving one tablespoon PMBS and ¼ cup citric acid to 5 gallons water is a good acid solution for a final barrel rinse. Add and swish the solution throughout to freshen and neutralize the barrel, then drain. The barrel is now ready for the wine.

After racking (see page 37) and before returning the wine to the barrel, rinse it three times by adding approximately 5 to 10 gallons of water and rocking the barrel back and forth to slosh out the debris. After the fresh water rinse, neutralize the barrel with the final acid rinse and drain.

If the barrel is to remain empty for any period of time, fill it halfway with water, add about 1 to 2 cups of Barrel-Kleen or other sodium percarbonate based solution, and allow it to sit overnight. Afterward, empty the barrel; rinse it 3 times then apply a final acid rinse and drain.

For short-term storage of 2 to 3 months, refill the barrel half way with water, add 1 ½ cup potassium metabisulfite and 1 cup citric acid (assuming the normal 55 to 60 gallon capacity), then fill the rest of the way with water. Occasionally top off the barrel with water to ensure full coverage. Change out this solution every three months.

Racking

After the wine is pressed and funneled into the wine container, solids and particles (i.e., dead yeast cells) suspended in the solution begin to precipitate out as the wine ages. *Racking* is the method used to separate the clear wine from the solids, or *lees* that settled in the carboy or barrel. The wine is siphoned or pumped off the lees and transferred to a clean food-grade plastic container. This major process step is critical for clarifying. Be sure to transfer the contents of all carboys or containers having the same wine into a single holding tank. Acid and/or SO_2 adjustments are made (if ML is complete) at this time to ensure consistency in the wine before returning to their sanitized containers.

I typically rack my wine three times. The first racking occurs three to four weeks after pressing to siphon the wine off the *gross lees*, which can contribute to unpleasant off-aromas (i.e., hydrogen-sulfide gas, or rotten egg smell) and developing bacteria. As the wine continues to clear, rack twice more or approximately every three to four months up to bottling.

While racking, wines will be exposed to the air which may cause white wines to oxidize, leading to discoloration or browning. Coat the wine with an inert gas to limit oxygen exposure during the racking process. Displace oxygen with the inert gas in newly cleaned, sanitized containers prior to transfer. Nitrogen and argon are the most common gases used in the industry and can be obtained from any welding supplier carrying compressed gases and dispensing apparatus (hoses and dispensing wands).

Conversely, oxidation of red wines can be helpful at racking. Allowing red wine to breathe during active oxygenation can potentially improve the nose and soften the palate. However, limit the amount of time spent in this environment. Inactive oxidation occurring in a barrel or carboy without SO_2 protection can result in the development of *acetaldehyde*, a condition associated with ethanol oxidation having a sherry-like character that can also be described as green apple or sour tastes. Acetaldehyde is also implicated in hangovers.

Simple racking equipment and methods

For small volumes, use the following equipment:

➢ One 6 to 8 foot raking hose ($^3/_8$" to $^1/_2$" in diameter)
➢ Racking wand or cane
➢ Wand cap

The hose fits directly on the crooked end of the wand. The wand cap fits at the tip of the wand to reduce the amount of sediment transferred to the secondary container. These products are available online or at any fermentation shop.

To rack, stick the sanitized racking wand into the carboy or vessel with the wand tip slightly above the lees. Suck on the racking hose to create a vacuum, then gravity siphon the clear wine into a food-grade plastic container. Dump and rinse the sediment from the carboy then clean and sanitize it before refilling. Make sure to refit the container with a fermentation lock if CO_2 action continues and allow a little air space in the neck for expansion. If secondary fermentation is complete, top off the container and seal it with a solid bung to limit oxidation.

For larger batches (i.e., barrels), use the following equipment:

> ➤ Two 6 to 8 foot 5/8" racking hoses complete with plastic garden hose fittings, purchased from any local hardware store.
> ➤ Small wine pump, available online or at your fermentation supply shop.

Attach the two sanitized hoses to the wine pump; tape a sanitized plastic rod to the sucking end of the hose, approximately three inches from the end. This allows pumping with minimum disturbance of the gross lees. Pump into a sanitized food-grade plastic holding vessel or agricultural tank. Dump the sediment from the barrel then rinse, rinse, rinse. Neutralize and freshen the barrel with the recommended SO_2/acid solution and drain. In the mean-time, make appropriate acid and SO_2 adjustments to the wine before returning to the newly cleaned barrel. Top off and refit the fermentation lock or solid nylon bung, depending on whether secondary (ML) fermentation is completed.

During both procedures, the lower tip of the racking cane or hose should be held midlevel and gradually lowered closer to the lees. This reduces the chances of stirring up the lees and transferring them to the holding tank.

If hydrogen sulfide (H_2S) is present in the carboy or barrel (rotten egg or permanent solution smell), lightly splash the wine during racking by placing your finger at the end of the siphon hose to create a gentle fan so the gases can dissipate as you rack. Follow through with a dose of SO_2 at the appropriate molecular levels to stabilize the wine (refer to post-fermentation SO_2 additions), <u>only</u> if ML is complete; if not, then add a light dose of SO_2 (less than < 10 ppm until ML is completed).

Bulk aging prior to bottling

Wine drinkers may appreciate a wine that is crisp and bright or soft and smooth. Once the vintner has obtained basic skill sets in winemaking, he or she can learn to make wine in the style that matches his or her taste. That's what makes this hobby so enjoyable and challenging.

During its initial stay in the barrel or carboy, the wine is considered "green" and needs to mellow out prior to bottling. As it rests, the wine goes through a form of chemical transformation that is reflected in its overall complexity. These changes include the linking of small tannic molecular chains to form longer chains that eventually precipitate out, reducing the harsh, young tannins. Using a neutral or new barrel is recommended for red wines because of its ability to breathe or *micro-oxygenate* the wine. Delicate flavors and a smoother mouth feel begin to develop as it ages in this type of container.

For white wines, consider bottling four or five months after bulk aging. For reds, one year to eighteen months; if, however, the tannins remain harsh, further barrel time or bulk aging may be required, depending on personal taste.

If barrel usage is considered, the micro-oxygenation process also leads to micro-transpiration or slight evaporation of the product inside. To avoid wine oxidation keep your barrels topped off. Wine oxidation can facilitate the growth of *Acetobacter*—a bacterium known to cause vinegar (ethyl acetate)—or other off-nose characteristic such as acetaldehyde. Make enough wine to fill your barrel and at least one or two carboys. This will ensure enough liquid to top off your barrel at racking and during evaporation. To limit oxidation in carboys, add a layer of nitrogen or argon in the headspace to purge out oxygen, or break down into smaller one-gallon jugs, making sure they're topped off.

> **Simple tip for topping barrels or carboys:** If a little wine is needed for topping, use a cheaper, clean commercial wine to top off. Because of the small amounts added, it doesn't affect the quality of the wine and could cost less than the product you're making.

Post-fermentation SO$_2$ adjustments

To avoid infection, a minimum level of SO$_2$ is necessary to stabilize the wine and inhibit the growth of wild yeast and bacteria after the primary and secondary fermentation. The most commonly asked question from beginning winemakers is how much SO_2 to add. There is one rule that, if followed, will maintain adequate levels of SO_2 in the wine during cellaring and before bottling.

SO_2 addition rule

This method is based on maintaining a molecular level of SO_2, since it is this molecular form that contains the most antimicrobial effect. The percentage of SO_2 is directly dependent on pH. Target a level of 0.8 ppm molecular SO_2 for white wine and 0.5 ppm for red wines. This is enough to provide effective antiseptic action to inhibit the growth of most microbes, as well as binds to acetaldehyde, in effect reducing off-nose characteristics attributed to oxidation.

You will need to know current free SO_2 levels before making any adjustments. However, first-time SO_2 additions are easy since we assume free levels are zero. Referring to Table 7 on page 43 (assuming a red wine with a pH value of 3.5), an addition of 25 ppm of free SO_2 is needed to achieve the desired molecular levels. Keep in mind that approximately 50% of the initial SO_2 inoculation will bind with other chemical elements in the wine, leaving the remaining 50% as free SO_2.

As you continue to monitor and adjust the free SO_2 levels, there become fewer unbound elements in the wine, making further additions of SO_2 more effective and needed less often. Check the free levels monthly and make appropriate adjustments. When in doubt, and without having any testing capability available, make your first big addition after malolactic fermentation is completed, then add 10 ppm of SO_2 each month thereafter, up to bottling.

Table 7 - Free SO$_2$ Levels

pH wine	Based on 0.8 molecular SO$_2$ (white wine)	Based on 0.5 molecular SO$_2$ (red wine)
Simple free SO$_2$ levels in wine - parts per million (ppm)		
3.0	13	8
3.1	16	10
3.2	21	13
3.3	26	16
3.4	32	20
3.5	40	25
3.6	50	31
3.7	63	39

The formula provided in Table 8 (page 44) calculates the appropriate dosage of SO$_2$ based on the free SO$_2$ needs of the wine. Measuring PMBS in the powdered form is the preferred method since it is used in many aspects of wine making and should be readily available to the home winemaker. Add the PMBS powder to wine drawn from the barrel or carboy and stir until fully dissolved, then incorporate this SO$_2$ solution back into the wine either at racking or directly into the wine container.

Checking and modifying the SO$_2$ level in your wine on a monthly basis prior to bottling is recommended for maintaining good health of the finished product.

Table 8 - Formula for Adding SO_2

Formula for addition of potassium metabisulfite (SO_2)
Calculation based on 0.00675 grams of potassium metabisulfite per gallon of wine
Or, (ppm)(0.00675) = grams/gallon

ppm Levels of SO_2 (refer to Table 7)	Grams of Potassium Metabisulfite per gallon of wine
70	0.4725
60	0.4050
50	0.3285
40	0.2700
30	0.2025
20	0.1350
10	0.0675

Note: Even though many home winemakers use Campden tablets that contain a premeasured amount of SO_2, discussions on techniques using PMBS powder are provided for the sake of simplicity. PMBS powder should be the number one item in every winemaker's arsenal for wine protection and sanitation.

How to check free SO_2 levels

There are two chemical analyses that can determine the amounts of free and total SO_2 in a wine: the Ripper method (described below) and the Aeration-Oxidation method. Both methods are fairly accurate but require some investment in laboratory equipment, chemical reagents, and a few laboratory skills. Until you realize that this is the hobby for you, three other approaches are:

> ➢ If available, use the services of a local wine lab to perform the SO_2 analysis.
> ➢ Get a mentor from your local wine club to help you.
> ➢ Ask your local wineries if they can perform these services (sometimes they do it for free).

Always keep meticulous records on wine tests, measurements, and additions. This way you'll always be aware of the total PMBS added to the wine.

Ripper method and modified Ripper method of determining SO_2 levels[7]

Total SO_2 present in wine comes in two forms: free and bound. Free levels of SO_2 act similar to white blood cells in the body by protecting the wine from infection, whereas SO_2 that is bound to acetaldehyde eliminates odors and tastes of oxidation in the solution.

---

[7] There are many variations of the Ripper method and modified Ripper method which are based on the wine sample size and the amount of reagents used. The methods described in this book are those that I use in my home winemaking operation.

Below are the essential lab equipment, supplies, and reagents needed to perform the Ripper titration method (available from any wine lab).

Laboratory Equipment:

> 250 mL Erlenmeyer flask (used to hold wine solution for titration)
> Burette (used to dispense reagents during titration)
> 20.0 mL volumetric pipette and 3 - 10.0 mL pipettes (used to transport a measured volume of liquid)

Reagents (available online from any wine lab):

> 0.02N iodine solution
> 1 + 3 sulfuric acid solution (corrosive)
> 1% starch solution
> 3% hydrogen peroxide
> wine or juice

Standard Ripper method

The standard Ripper method is used to measure the level of SO_2 in wines, allowing the typical wine sample to be tested within a few minutes. The equipment necessary to perform this test is relatively inexpensive, making this test attractive to home winemakers as well.

The basic principle of the Ripper titration method is to determine SO_2 through titration with the iodine solution. The Ripper method is dedicated in determining the "free" SO_2 available.

Instructions for determining free SO_2

> - Step 1: Pipette 20 mL of wine into a 250 mL conical flask.
> - Step 2: Add 10 mL sulfuric acid.
> - Step 3: Add 3 mL of 1% starch solution.
> - Step 4: Fill burette with 0.02N iodine solution.

Titration is the gradual adding of controlled and measured amounts of a solution (in this case, iodine) into another solution (the combination of wine, sulfuric acid, and starch) to obtain a reaction (change in color). Titration is complete once the reaction between the two solutions stops (color change has stabilized). The measured amount added is calculated into a value that denotes a concentration of a substance in the solution (i.e., sulfur dioxide) levels.

In this case a dark purple color appears when adding the iodine to the solution containing starch. Sulfuric acid is added to lower the pH of the solution in order to neutralize the bound SO_2, thereby limiting this test to "free" SO_2 only. At the point that color change no longer occurs, titration is completed.

> - Step 5: Document the amount of iodine in the burette (start point) and begin adding a small amount of the calibrated iodine from the burette to the solution (one drop at a time).

As this occurs the iodine reacts with the water in the wine, SO_2, and the sulfuric acid, forming hydrogen iodide until all iodine is consumed. Each drop of iodine that is added decreases the SO_2 and water in the solution and slightly increases the sulfuric acid and hydrogen iodide.

Continue adding iodine to the solution drop by drop until the color no longer changes. At this point, a small amount of residual iodine remains behind and is no longer completely consumed. This is because SO_2 is no longer in the solution to react to the iodine. It is at this point that titration is complete and the end point has been reached and the amount of SO_2 can be calculated.

> **Step 6: Measure the amount of milliliters left in the burette (end point). Subtract this number from the start point documented in Step 5 to determine the amount of iodine used during titration.**

> **Step 7: Calculate free SO_2 using the following formula: Free SO_2 (mg/l) = 32 × mL of iodine used.** Example: If 1.2 mL of iodine is used then the amount of SO_2 in the wine is estimated at 38.4 ppm (32 × 1.2 mL = 38.4).

Using this method can produce some errors, especially when determining color change. It is recommended that these steps be repeated for each wine sample in order to validate the results. Also, this method can be skewed when testing red wines, since some of the iodine reacts to other phenolic compounds, such as pigment, and can cause errors anywhere between 5 and 20 ppm. Retesting the wine using the modified Ripper method can diminish this problem.

The modified Ripper method

The modified Ripper method helps to identify iodine that is consumed by these compounds. With this method a second solution sample is measured (using Steps 1 through 3 above) and 5 mL of 3% hydrogen peroxide is added to remove all free SO_2 from the sample, leaving only the phenolic materials to be tested. Repeat Step 5 until titration is complete. Repeat Steps 6 and 7 to calculate the phenolic compounds in the solution (e.g., if 0.2 mL of iodine is used, the amount of these materials is measured at 6.4 ppm (32 times 0.2mL = 6.4)).

> **Step 8: Subtract the results of the modified Ripper method from the Ripper method to determine free SO_2 levels (e.g., 38.4 ppm – 6.4 ppm = 32 ppm free SO_2).**

To summarize, the following steps are taken to measure free SO_2 in red wine:

> Measure free SO_2 using the standard Ripper method.
> Measure a second sample treated with hydrogen peroxide (modified Ripper method).
> Subtract result from the second measurement from the first measurement to obtain free SO_2 only without the interaction between SO_2 and the phenolic compounds.

Simple SO_2 definitions - There are three types of SO_2 of concern, including:
> Total SO_2 – reflects total free and bound levels of SO_2.
> Free SO_2 – unbound portion of SO_2. This measurement and the pH determine the molecular levels of SO_2 in your wine.
> Molecular SO_2 – level of SO_2 molecules available for antimicrobial action that responds to other molecules to reduce oxidation (i.e., 0.5 ppm [molecular] for a red, and 0.8 ppm for a white).

Oak additions

Oak helps to fix color and add complexity to a finished red wine, as well, most wine connoisseurs agree that oak plays an important role in adding aroma, flavor, and structure to wine. Personal taste dictates the amount of oak flavors or character to add. Some wine enthusiasts prefer a fruit forward young wine with no oak addition but the majority of wine drinkers prefer some oak character.

In the current commercial and home winemaking market there is a myriad of oak products to choose from, the most common being the oak barrel. Besides the American barrel, a large number of barrels are imported from France, Hungary and Yugoslavia.

As a home winemaker, I use neutral barrels, which can be purchased from your local winery. Neutral means that it will no longer impart an oak flavor in the wine; however, it serves two additional purposes:

> Barrels are large enough to hold 60 gallons of wine.
> Barrels breathe and naturally micro-oxygenate the wine. This controlled oxidation process changes the flavor and texture of wine, and eventually mellows it.

Most commercial wineries will bulk age and later blend red wines from a combination of new, one-year-old, two-year-old, and neutral barrels. This allows for the benefits of micro-oxygenating the wine without the overwhelming presence of wood, tannin, and vanilla flavors derived from a new barrel.

There are many oak products available online or at your local fermentation store that effectively add oak character to your finished wine, including:

> Oak powder
> Oak spirals
> Oak chips
> Oak beans
> Oak staves
> Oak balls

These products are usually derived from French and American oak and are easily used in most wine storage containers, including carboys, stainless steel, and neutral barrels. Place a measured amount in your wine container (as recommended by the manufacturer), wait for the desired aroma and taste to develop, and then remove by racking.

For oak additions during bulk aging, use a product shape that can be easily added or extracted from the narrow hole of the carboy or barrel. Nylon mesh bags are good for suspending oak spirals and staves in barrels and can be easily removed without racking as long as a fishing line is attached. Oak chips, beans, or balls are good for use in carboys. After oak extraction, rack the wine off the smaller oak particles, wash out the container and then sanitize, rinse, and refill. Adding two to four ounces of oak product per five gallons of finished wine is often recommended.

To avoid contamination, it is important to sanitize your selected oak product before adding it to the finished wine. To sanitize: add $^1/_{16}$ teaspoon PMBS to one gallon of non-chlorinated water. Soak the product in this solution for about thirty minutes.

Optional Practices

Clarification – fining, filtering, and cold stabilization

Wine clarifies as it sits and ages in bulk storage. During this natural process, suspended particles and dead yeast cells precipitate out in the form of lees at the bottom of the container. The wine is then racked off the lees and transferred to a sanitized container. In many younger white wines, the beginning winemaker can opt to speed up the stabilization process, either through fining or filtration.

Fining

Fining is the process of cleaning haze, tannin harshness, or protein matter from a wine using chemical or natural substances or *fining agent*. The fining agent is stirred into the wine and allowed to settle. These substances consist of natural or synthesized proteins that attract electrochemically with positive charges to other proteins or solids in the wines that are negatively charged. Ultimately they attract to each other and precipitate out.

If fining agents are considered, it is important to use the minimum dosage recommended by the manufacturer. Excess amounts of these agents can strip out important polyphenols that affect taste, color, and mouth feel. Be sure to read all manufacturers' specifications prior to using fining products.

The two most common fining agents used by winemakers are bentonite and egg whites, which are used and prepared as follows:

Bentonite for fining

Bentonite is used in white wine to stabilize and eliminate protein haze.

Add 3 tablespoons bentonite to 16 ounces of boiling water. Using a blender at medium speed, mix the ingredients for about two minutes until creamy and then allow the mixture to stand in the refrigerator overnight. One to two table-spoons of this mixture is used to clarify one gallon of wine.

Thoroughly stir the solution throughout the wine using a carboy or barrel stirring rod to insure full suspension. Bentonite can be added after fermentation; however, adding bentonite during fermentation is considered more effective since the solution is continuously roiled throughout the wine as it ferments.

Egg whites for fining

Egg whites are used in red wines to reduce heavy tannins and harshness.

Use ½ egg white per 5-gallon carboy or 4 to 6 egg whites per barrel. Separate the egg white(s) from the yolk, add a pinch of salt, and whisk to a smooth mixture with no froth.

Pour the egg white solution into the wine while stirring to distribute the solution throughout. Allow one to two weeks for the solution to settle then rack off and bottle. Note: If the solution is prepared correctly, there is no risk of salmonella since these bacteria will only form in the egg yolk.

Filtration

Filtration is ideal for achieving a competition ready wine in terms of clarity, but does not enhance the aroma or taste. Some say that as in fining, there is a risk of losing desirable phenolic flavor along with those less desirable solids. Fining is also considered less harsh than filtration since it mimics the natural clarification process at an accelerated rate.

There are many filtration devices available to the small family winery, the most popular of which is the Buon Vino SuperJet. This device offers three grades (micron sizes) of single-use filter pads of cellulose fibers, including coarse, medium, and fine. Ask your wine club if a filter is available to its members.

In most cases a coarse filter pad would be used before a medium or fine pad since it would eliminate the large particles suspended in the wine without clogging. However, for red wine that is properly racked and clear, using a medium grade filter at the onset would be fine. For white wines, filtering should be performed in stages starting with the coarse grade, then later to medium, then fine. Allow at least five days between filtration. Make sure the filter pump is prepped and sanitized prior to usage, following the manufacturer's specifications for the product. Soak the pads in a bucket of clean non-chlorinated water for about 10 minutes and then place them in the filtering system. You are now ready to clarify your wine.

Once filtering begins, refrain from turning the pump on and off until filtering is complete. The filter pad relaxes between pump starts, and cellulose fibers and sedimentation will be pulled into the wine, causing a haze of particles two to three weeks after bottling. This is particularly noticeable in white wine.

As you begin filtering from your holding tank (carboy or barrel), you will notice water flowing from the filter pads. Pump this into a dump bucket until wine begins to flow, and then move the hose to your final holding tank or bottling container without stopping the pump.

Cold stabilization

There are many types of acids contained in wine, including tartaric, malic, and citric. It is the tartaric acid that can be identified as crystals floating in white wines when held up to the light (in the form of potassium bitartrates) or can be found clinging to the cork in both reds and whites. This is solely a cosmetic issue that does affect flavor, but may be considered a flaw when competitively judged.

Most tartaric crystals bind with the lees during clarification and are extracted from the wine during the racking process. The remaining soluble bitartrate remains hidden in the wine until it is exposed to temperature change. Once lower temperatures come into play the soluble bitartrates begin to crystallize and can be seen floating in the wine.

Cold stabilization is the method used to correct this problem. During cold stabilization, the wine is exposed to low temperatures for approximately 10 days. During this period, tartaric crystals begin to form and attach to the sides of the container. The wine is then racked off the crystals into another container, topped off, and sealed.

Methods to cold stabilize include exposure to cold temperatures, either naturally in cold climate areas, or mechanically using a freezer or kegerator. Make sure the temperature is at or below 31° but not too cold. Extreme temperatures can cause other problems if the wine is allowed to freeze, especially if using a glass carboy. This could break the carboy through expansion and jeopardize its contents.

Not all commercial winemakers opt to filter, fine, or stabilize their wines. As a beginning first year winemaker consider skipping this step. Wine has an uncanny ability of taking care of itself given the right conditions and given time to allow it to process naturally. I believe the more you handle or touch the wine, the more you toy with its natural aromas and character. During your first year keep the winemaking process as simple and easy as possible to ensure a good outcome.

Chapter 5 - Blending, Bottling, Storing, and Final Aging

Wine will tell you when it's ready

Everyone has their own unique pH and acid makeup that affects the way they perceive taste. This is why the appreciation of wine is subjective and personal to each individual. Blending is a way to customize a wine to one's preferences.

Summer blending and customizing

Summer blending is the time to ask:

- ➤ Do you like your wine?
- ➤ Can the wine be improved through blending?
- ➤ How much do we blend?

These questions can be answered through blending bench trials. Blending requires the mixing of two or more wines, either the same or different varietals for purposes of enhancing or correcting the character of the finished product. Blending customizes a product that appeals to the winemaker. Usually it involves the blending of compatible varietals (i.e., those varietals that create Super Tuscans, Rhone, Bordeaux, and Chianti blends), or fixing off-balanced wine.

The best way to conduct a blending trial is through the blind tasting process, working with family and friends to taste and compare different wine combinations to determine the final blend.

Simple rule for blending: Do not blend a flawed wine having oxidation, *Brettanomyces*, or other properties (refer to *Common Wine Defects*). By chasing the bad after good the outcome will always be disappointing.

Aging

Aging is the process of various tannins responding physically with other elements and components in the wine until they are unable to stay in the solution and precipitate out. Tannins come from either the grapes themselves (skins and seeds) or from being aged in oak. Grape tannins are preferred over oak when it comes to aging, so grapes like big reds (Petite Syrah or Cabernet) with thicker skins will have better aging potential.

Ultimately, the best grape is one having a perfect balance of tannin, fruit, and acid, resulting in the best vintages for aging. A good grape is one that requires very little adjustment in the initial and post-fermentation processes.

The aging process occurs mostly in the first six to twelve months of cellaring as precipitates are eliminated through the racking, fining, and final filtration processes. After bottling, bouquets of the aged wine (reductive aromas) replace the initial aromas of the fruit, and the color in red wine lightens as the red pigments bond and become sediment. This sediment is not a flaw and typically indicates a mature wine. In the event of sediment decant the wine prior to serving.

Wines vary from young, fruity, and tannic wines to an aged wine with a softer mouth feel, less fruity, and generally more complex and subtle in taste. Some assume that the longer wine ages, the better it gets. However, not all wine must age. It depends on the varietal and the wine itself. Some like acidic, tart white wines versus those who prefer a softer, somewhat smoother red. This is what makes this hobby so interesting in terms of customizing your product.

Simple facts on aging wine:

> ➢ You cannot make a good wine from a mediocre grape.
> ➢ Wine must have fairly high levels of tannin to age.
> ➢ A good wine should maintain a proper pH/acid balance for freshness.

Bottling

Sanitize any used bottles with the following steps:

> ➢ Place bottles in the kitchen sink filled with warm water and 1 cup of ammonia.
> ➢ Remove stains inside using a bottle brush, then rinse thoroughly to eliminate residue.
> ➢ Run upside down in a dishwasher set at "sanitation," without using detergent.
> ➢ After the hot dry cycle, remove bottles and place them upside down in a clean wine box lined with newspaper.

You can avoid this process if you choose to purchase new bottles.

Final bottle preparation is done at the bottling site using a bottle tree and rinser. The bottle tree is a sturdy plastic unit with pegs designed to hold up to 90 bottles. A rinser is a sprayer containing a reservoir to hold PMBS sanitation solution and an upright spray nozzle to apply the solution inside the bottle, after which the bottle is placed upside down on the tree to dry.

There are various ways to fill bottles, depending on volume and budget. The cheapest way is to bottle directly from the bulk storage container (i.e., carboy, keg, or barrel) using gravity feed. This can be done with a sanitized racking tube and hose clamp designed to stop the flow of wine between bottles. For larger batches, you may use a multi-station bottle filler. This unit has a reservoir to hold the wine, a float valve to keep the wine from overflowing, plungers to fill the bottles, and adjustable shelves to control the fill level in the neck of the bottle. Make sure there is a small space between the wine and the cork to allow for expansion in the bottle. Corking the bottle can be done using an inexpensive handheld corker or bench model corking machine that is designed for larger jobs.

Before bottling, make sure to:

> Sanitize all bottling equipment using the Five-Step Cleaning Rules.
> Ensure SO_2 ranges in the finished wine are at appropriate molecular levels.
> Use new sulfated corks to avoid contamination.

Temperature

Wines that are improperly stored can be expected to age and fall apart more quickly, so try keeping your wine at or around 55° F. If this is not possible, store your wine in a dark closet or basement where temperatures are not expected to fluctuate. Make sure to taste a bottle every so often to track its progress.

Bottle sickness a.k.a. bottle-shock

All wine goes through a period of bottle-shock or sickness. This short-term phenomenon is attributed to the wine being exposed to oxygen, causing a chemical reaction with various elements of the wine. The time it takes the wine to fully integrate the oxygen in the solution and "settle down" is considered the "shock" or "sickness" period. During this time the wine tastes significantly different than it did prior to bottling. DO NOT PANIC! Resting the wine two to six months after bottling is usually enough time to repair the flavors. Many wineries will not consider releasing a product until at least six months to a year after bottling.

Dumb phase

Also common during aging is when the wine slips into a "dumb" period or phase where flavors and aromas are subdued and understated. Soon after the initial bottle-shock phase has passed, the wine may begin to taste rich, jammy, and full of good flavors and aromas. However, be prepared when the wine begins to shut down again and taste off-character. Don't be alarmed. You have to be willing to wait it out; sometimes the "dumb" phase cannot be predicted.

Chapter 6 - Simple Things to Consider

Vintage year one

Set realistic expectations in the first year while learning about grape quality, acid, and sugar balancing. It may not be a $20 bottle of wine. Perhaps the wine is slightly acidic or may contain off aromas due to cellar management or the lack of adequate SO_2 levels. Don't be alarmed, and don't give up! It's a learning experience, and with each subsequent year and batch you'll learn more and grow.

Read winemaking magazines, join a wine club, find a mentor. If you cannot solve a problem using this book, research other ways to address it. Seek advice from commercial wineries or through professional wine labs. Your skills will improve with time and experience. You'll learn the importance of a balanced must and the significance of sanitizing your equipment and maintaining a clean, healthy environment.

Always start with the fruit, for your wine will only be as good as the grape you choose. A quality, somewhat balanced fruit from a properly maintained vineyard will not require major tweaking. It will become what it is destined to be without much interference. Whenever possible, buy good grapes, slightly adjust, and step away from the natural process.

Step out of your comfort zone

Experiment a little. With each vintage, incorporate one or more new products or methods to your winemaking arsenal, such as using new yeast strains or nutrients, enzymes for color extraction, or oak additions. Read winemaking magazines and journals in order to stay abreast of the latest trends in this dynamic industry. Take an annual trip to your favorite fermentation supply shop just prior to harvest to check out the new product lines. Obtain fermentation product catalogs and handbooks from industry leaders such as Lallemand, Scott Laboratories, and Vinquiry.

Relationships with the growers

Choose your grower wisely, one who manages grapes from start to finish, ensuring the best quality product. Once a commercial winemaker finds a premium grape source, he/she will establish an ongoing relationship with the farmer for consistency of each vintage. Normally, a commercial winemaker's reputation is based on the quality, taste, and character of the wine that appeals to the customer. This style, however, is not only reflective of the winemaker's skills and personal taste, but also reflects the personality and character of the farmer. The farmer's skills in cultivating, trellising, fertilizing, and spraying are just as essential in developing a fine wine.

The farmer knows that by trellising a plant to maintain the proper canopy for proper sunlight and shade and providing the maximum airflow allows the fruit to develop and mature consistently throughout the orchard. Thinning each plant ensures the premium quality of the fruit, decreases disease and rot, and increases the overall price per pound of the product grown. Although some seasonal and vineyard variations may occur (e.g., weather conditions) it remains in your favor when you choose your grapes and grower wisely.

Join a club

The purpose of most home winemaking associations is to organize, conduct, and attend discussions, lectures, field trips, experiments, and demonstrations regarding all aspects of grape growing and winemaking. Most are nonprofit, informational, educational programs that promote the art of winemaking, with a specific emphasis on members helping members. Annual dues are assessed to ensure membership. Dues are used to promote winemaking, purchase equipment for club member use, and fund educational seminars.

Last words

The science and chemistry of winemaking can be intimidating, but the experience and rewards make it well worth the effort. As you progress you will find that winemaking becomes irresistible and pulls you in with a preoccupation shared by many. At harvest time you become Pavlov's dog and salivate over the year's prospects. You ponder on sugar, pH and acid levels, and pore over fermentation supply catalogs for the best yeast or enzyme additions.

Anticipation of the next year's harvest stimulates discussion through the exchange of ideas surrounding winemaking techniques with other winemakers. Quality life experiences are created by the heightened awareness of nature and the environment within the vineyard, the application of life sciences and chemistry, and the savoring of fine foods with wine pairings. The most important thing to remember is that all aspects of winemaking are better shared. Whether it's the crush, racking, cellaring or bottling, celebrating life with family and friends is the ultimate reward.

Appendix 1: Quick Reference Crush to Cellar Check-off List

This check-off list guides the reader step-by-step through the winemaking process.

Crush Stage

☑ Crush stage - Chapter 1	Comments
☐ Crush	Crush red grapes and transfer to an open primary fermenter. Crush white grapes and immediately send to the press.
☐ Press and Settle – White Grapes	After pressing allow white grapes to settle for 12 hours. Rack the clear juice from the gross lees and transfer to an open primary fermenter.
☐ Measure and Adjust	Measure and adjust sugar, pH, and acid levels (Chapter 3), and document your findings (Appendix 6).
☐ Stabilize	Stabilize the must by adding 3.1g of potassium metabisulfite (PMBS) per 10 gallons of must to kill spoilage yeasts and bacteria.

Pre-Fermentation Stage

☑ Pre-Fermentation Stage – Chap. 2 & 3	Comments
☐ **Measure and Adjust**	Measure the must sugar levels again and adjust, if necessary. This allows for rehydration of raisins.
☐ **Enzyme Addition (Optional)**	Add Opti-Red or other brand enzyme for color and juice extraction 12 hours after stabilization – dosage based on product specification.
☐ **Yeast Nutrient - DAP**	Add DAP for additional yeast nutrient 12 hours after stabilization – dosage based on product specification.
☐ **Yeast Inoculation**	Rehydrate selected yeast strain and inoculate the must.
☐ **Oak Powder Addition (Optional)**	One to two pounds of oak powder per 1,000 pounds of grapes or 10 to 20 grams per gallon of must – enhances the overall wine quality without imparting oak flavor.
☐ **Fermentation Nutrient**	Add powder fermentation nutrient, at $^1/_3$ intervals at the onset of fermentation. If using time-release tablets, add one time at the beginning of the fermentation.

Fermentation Stage

☑ Fermentation Stage – Chap. 2 & 3	Comments
☐ Cover Primary Fermenter	Cover lightly with food-grade plastic to avoid fruit fly contamination.
☐ Check Temperature	Check must temperature daily to avoid overheating (90°+). Cool with frozen water bottles, if necessary.
☐ Check Specific Gravity (Brix)	Check Brix daily to determine nutrient additions ($^1/_3$ intervals) and conclusion of fermentation.
☐ Punch the Cap – Red Wine Only	Punch the cap three times per day – for must health and color extraction.
☐ Malolactic Fermentation – Red Wine	Inoculate with freeze-dried ML culture at the end of the fermentation.
☐ Press	Press must at 2° Brix or below; pump juice into sanitized secondary fermentation containers.

Cellaring Stage

☑ Cellaring – Chapter 4	Comments
☐ Secondary Fermentation	Check ML progress using chromatography paper, or have it professionally tested.
☐ Clean	Clean and sanitize all equipment and tubing before and after each procedure.
☐ First Racking	Pump juice off gross lees 3 to 4 weeks after pressing and transfer to a clean container. Always top off container to avoid oxidation.
☐ Measure and Adjust	Measure and adjust pH and acid levels and document. If ML is completed, add first addition of PMBS to stabilize the wine. Maintain SO_2 levels at 0.8 molecular for white wine and 0.5 molecular for red.
☐ Oak Addition	Add oak adjuncts to taste.
☐ Second Racking	Pump juice off fine lees 3 months after the first racking and transfer to a clean container; top off.
☐ Measure and Adjust	Final pH and acid adjustment, if needed. Maintain SO_2 levels.
☐ Third Racking	Pump juice off fine lees 3 months after the second racking. Check SO_2 levels and top off.
☐ Bottle	Filter and bottle into clean, sanitized containers when the wine is ready.

Appendix 2: Quick Reference for Measuring Total Active Acid

Maintaining proper total active acid (TA) levels is crucial for a healthy fermentation and overall balance of the finished wine. High TA will result in wines having a tart, rough finish; low TA creates a more dull and lethargic wine. White wines with a TA value of 0.65% to 0.75% and red wines with a TA value of 0.60% to 0.70% are considered to be in balance.

The pH is a measure of the acid strength in the solution. The higher the pH value the lower the acidity level; conversely, the lower the pH value the higher the acid. The pH is easily measured using a pH meter. Typically a good pH range for a dry white wine is 3.1 to 3.4, while the pH range for a dry red wine is 3.3 to 3.6.

There are two simple methods for measuring total acid (TA) or acid strength; both are done with a pH meter.

Simple Method Number One - Measuring pH

> After calibration, place the pH meter into a small amount of grape juice and document your findings.
> Is it within the typical pH values for red wines (3.3 and 3.6 pH)?
> If yes, then the pre-fermentation solution should have a good acid balance.
> If not, then the solution may need adjusting (refer to Chapter 3 - Simple Tip for Acid Adjustments Based on pH Readings).

The chart below defines wine characteristics that are directly affected by certain pH levels[8]:

Wine Characteristic	Low pH Range (3.0 - 3.4)	High pH Range (3.6 - 4.0)
Oxidation	Less Oxidation	More Oxidation
Amount of color	More	Less
Kind of color	Ruby	Browner
Yeast fermentation	Unaffected	Unaffected
Protein stability	More Stable	Less Stable
Bacterial growth	Less	More
Bacterial fermentation	Less	More

Simple Method Number Two – Measuring TA

Essential tools needed to measure TA include: a 10 mL pipette, a 10 mL syringe, a pH meter, and a wine glass. Essential chemicals and reagents include: 4.1 pH and 7.1 pH buffer solutions for pH meter calibration and a bottle of 0.1 Normality (N) sodium hydroxide. After tools and reagents are gathered and the pH meter is calibrated the winemaker will perform the following:

➤ Using a 10 mL pipette, measure out 10 mL of grape juice into a clean wine glass.

---

[8] Table on wine characteristics based on certain pH levels is taken from *The Home Winemakers Manual, by Lum Eisenman, 1999,* and other on-line sources.

- ➤ Place the calibrated pH meter into this measured sample solution.
- ➤ Fill a 10 mL syringe with 0.1N sodium hydroxide[9] (NaOH).
- ➤ Slowly add 0.1N solution, 1 mL at a time, watching the pH meter. Thoroughly mix the solution by swirling the glass.
- ➤ Once the pH meter registers 6.0 pH the pH meter reading will begin to accelerate; add only 0.1 to 0.5 mL NaOH beyond this point.
- ➤ As soon as the meter registers and holds at 8.2 pH, determine the amount of NaOH used by subtracting the end point (say 2.5 mL) from the start point of 10 mL = 7.5 mL
- ➤ Gather the data from the process above and fill in the following formula:

$$[(mL\ NaOH) \times (Normality\ of\ NaOH) \times (0.075) \times (100)] \div (mL\ in\ the\ wine\ sample)$$

Or

$$[(7.5) \times (0.1) \times (0.075) \times (100)] \div 10\ mL$$

Or

$$5.625 \div 10\ mL = 0.56\%\ TA$$

- ➤ Repeat this process twice to get the average measurement.

---

[9] Sodium hydroxide has the tendency to draw moisture from the air, and will throw off future acid test results. Seal and store this reagent in the refrigerator right after testing.

Is the solution within typical acid values for red wines (between 0.6% and 0.7% total acid)? If yes, then your pre-fermentation solution should have a good acid balance. If no, then the grape solution should be adjusted (see Chapter 3).

Appendix 3: Quick Reference for Sugar Adjustments

As fall approaches, farmers begin to assess their crop for signs of ripeness. Sugar is tested for alcohol potential and acid for drinkability and shelf life. It is hoped that when harvested, sugar and acid levels are in sync to achieve optimum wine balance. Unfortunately, these two elements rarely cooperate. Crops subject to hot weather may spike sugars to ideal conditions, but may not be ripe, resulting in high acetic wines. These same crops, left to mature, may have elevated sugar levels, making fermentation difficult and resulting in high alcohol and residual sweetness.

This section describes the process of reducing sugars in the grape juice prior to fermentation in order to achieve good alcohol balance. Sugar additions will not be discussed since this process is designed to bolster the alcohol potential of a lesser quality, unripe fruit. As mentioned earlier, you cannot make a quality wine choosing substandard grapes.

Not all grapes high in sugar are inferior; in fact some are known to produce delicious, full-bodied wines; however, fermenting high fructose grapes increases the risks in fermentation. High Brix = high alcohol, which is the most common preventable factor in stuck fermentations. Elevated alcohol will kill most yeast strains and prevent the must from going dry, resulting in a "late harvest" style wine containing residual sugars. If you like a sweet, high alcoholic wine, that's fine; if not, you need to reduce the sugars.

The easiest way to reduce sugar is with water (amelioration). You may be concerned that diluting the must will result in a watered down wine, but this is not the case. Typically, grapes picked with high sugar values are dehydrated. Adding water simply rehydrates the fruit without compromising wine quality.

Use a hydrometer to calculate the future alcohol potential of the wine. The hydrometer is a sealed, hand-blown glass tube having a lead-weighted ballast in the bottom bulb and calibrated scales (i.e., specific gravity and °Brix scale) in the upper stem. The hydrometer comes with a tall test cylinder that, when filled with juice, allows the hydrometer to float freely.

The higher the density of the juice the higher soluble solids or sugar are present. Initial °Brix is identified on this scale as the hydrometer floats. Potential % of alcohol by volume is found by multiplying the known °Brix by a factor of 0.56. For example, grapes measuring at 25.5° Brix will achieve potential alcohol of 14.28% (25.5 × 0.56). For best results target a potential alcohol level between 13.5% and 14.5%, or Brix values between 24.1° Brix and 25.9° Brix.

Using the chart on page 79, determine the amount of non-chlorinated water needed to achieve 24.5° Brix in the must—the ideal sugar level for winemaking. For example (as highlighted): 1,000 lb of grapes comes in at 29.5° Brix. This would require approximately 16.0 gallons of non-chlorinated water to achieve the desired target of 24.5° Brix. If you desire higher alcohol, add less water and retest using the hydrometer to achieve your objective.

Simple Water Addition Matrix

Gallons of water added to grape must (based on weight) -
Assumes final sugars at approximately 24.5° Brix (+ or −)

°Brix at Harvest	Approx. Alcohol	1,000 Lb	500 Lb	200 Lb	100 Lb
25.0	14.5%	2.0	1.0	0.4	0.2
25.5	14.8%	3.0	1.5	0.6	0.3
26.0	15.1%	5.0	2.5	1.0	0.5
26.5	15.4%	6.0	3.0	1.2	0.6
27.0	15.7%	8.0	4.0	1.6	0.8
27.5	16.0%	9.0	4.5	1.8	0.9
28.0	16.2%	10.0	5.0	2.0	1.0
28.5	16.5%	12.0	6.0	2.4	1.2
29.0	16.8%	14.0	7.0	2.8	1.4
29.5	17.1%	16.0	8.0	3.2	1.6
30.0	17.4%	17.0	8.5	3.4	1.7
30.5	17.7%	18.0	9.0	3.6	1.8
31.0	18.0%	20.0	10.0	4.0	2.0
31.5	18.3%	22.0	11.0	4.4	2.2
32.0	18.6%	23.0	11.5	4.6	2.3

Adding water to the must will do two things: dilute the sugar concentration and reduce the total acidity. Unless the must already has excessive acid, it is important to acidulate the water with tartaric acid before adding to the must in order to maintain current TA and pH levels. The general rule is to add 6 grams of tartaric acid per liter, or approximately 22.5 grams per gallon of non-chlorinated water.

As with acid additions, it is wise to add about half of the targeted water addition during the rehydration process. Punch the must well and recheck the sugars with the hydrometer in a few hours. If raisins are present, sugars will be extracted as they become rehydrated. This extraction may bump up the sugar level as the must sits. Adding half the water in the beginning gives the winemaker a better picture of the true sugars that need to be adjusted.

Appendix 4: Quick Reference for Potassium Metabisulfite (SO₂) Testing

Ripper Method and Modified Ripper Method of Determining SO$_2$ Level

Total sulfur dioxide (SO$_2$) present in wine comes in two forms: free and bound. Free levels of SO$_2$ act similar to white blood cells in the body by protecting the wine from infection, whereas SO$_2$ that is bound to acetaldehyde eliminates odors and tastes of oxidation in the solution.

Below is a list of essential lab equipment, supplies, and reagents needed to perform the Ripper titration method.

Laboratory Equipment:

➢ 250 mL Erlenmeyer flask
➢ burette
➢ 20.0 mL volumetric pipette
➢ 3 - 10.0 mL pipettes

Reagents (available online from any wine lab):

➢ 0.02N iodine solution
➢ 1 + 3 sulfuric acid solution (corrosive)
➢ 1% starch solution
➢ 3% hydrogen peroxide
➢ wine or juice

The standard Ripper method is used to measure the level of SO$_2$ in wine, allowing the typical wine sample to be tested within a few minutes. Additionally, the equipment necessary to perform this test is relatively inexpensive, making this test attractive to home winemakers.

The basic principle of the Ripper titration method is to determine SO_2 through titration with the iodine solution. The Ripper method is used to determine the "free" SO_2 available.

Instructions for determining free SO_2:

> **Step 1: Pipette 20 mL of wine into a 250 mL Erlenmeyer flask.**
> **Step 2: Add 10 mL sulfuric acid.**
> **Step 3: Add 3 mL of 1% starch solution.**
> **Step 4: Fill burette with 0.02N iodine solution.**

Titration is the gradual addition of controlled and measured amounts of a solution (in this case iodine) into another solution (the combination of wine, sulfuric acid, and starch) to obtain a reaction (change in color). Titration is complete once the reaction between the two solutions stops (color change has stabilized). The measured amount added can then be calculated into a value that denotes a concentration of a substance in the solution (i.e., SO_2 levels).

In this case a dark purple color appears when adding the iodine to the solution containing starch.[10] Sulfuric acid is added to lower the pH of the solution in order to neutralize the bound SO_2, thereby limiting this test to "free" SO_2 only.

---

[10] You may consider using a yellow "bug light" to help in detecting color change. Use a flexible utility lamp to focus the light directly on the solution as you titrate.

At the point that color change no longer occurs, titration is completed.

> **Step 5: Document the amount of iodine in the burette (start point) and begin adding a small amount of the calibrated iodine from the burette to the solution (one drop at a time).**

As this occurs the iodine reacts with the water in the wine, the SO_2, and the sulfuric acid, forming hydrogen iodide until all iodine is consumed. Each drop of iodine that is added decreases the SO_2 and water in the solution and slightly increases the sulfuric acid and hydrogen iodide.

Continue adding iodine to the solution drop by drop until the color no longer changes. At this point, a small amount of residual iodine remains behind and is no longer completely consumed. This is because SO_2 is no longer in the solution to react to the iodine. It is at this point that titration is complete and the end point has been reached and the amount of SO_2 can be calculated.

> **Step 6: Measure the amount of milliliters left in the burette (end point). Subtract this number from the start point documented in Step 5 to determine the amount of iodine used during titration.**
> **Step 7: Calculate free SO_2 using the following formula: Free SO_2 (mg/l) = 32 × mL of iodine used. Example**: If 1.2 mL of iodine is used then the amount of SO2 in the wine is estimated at 38.4 ppm (32 × 1.2 mL = 38.4).

Using this method can produce some errors, especially when determining color change. It is recommended that these steps be repeated for each wine sample in order to validate the results. Also, this method can be skewed when testing red wines, since some of the iodine reacts to other phenolic compounds, such as pigment, and can cause errors anywhere between 5 and 20 ppm. This problem can be diminished by re-testing the wine using the modified Ripper method.

The modified Ripper method helps to identify iodine that is consumed by the phenolic compounds. With this method a second solution sample is measured (using Steps 1 through 3 above). However, 5 mL of 3% hydrogen peroxide is added to remove all free SO_2 from the sample, leaving only the phenolic materials to be tested. Accordingly, repeat Step 5 until titration is complete. Repeat Steps 6 and 7 to calculate the phenolic compounds in the solution. **Example:** If 0.2 mL of iodine is used, the amount of these materials is measured at 6.4 ppm (32 × 0.2 mL = 6.4).

> **Step 8: Subtract the results of the modified Ripper method from the Ripper method to determine free SO_2 levels. Example: 38.4 ppm – 6.4 ppm = 32 ppm free SO_2.**

To summarize, the following steps are taken to measure free SO_2 in red wine:

> Measure free SO_2 using the standard Ripper method.
> Measure a second sample treated with hydrogen peroxide (modified Ripper method).
> Subtract result from the second measurement from the first measurement to obtain free SO_2 only without the interaction between SO_2 and the phenolic compounds.

Having low levels of SO_2 is a common mistake, but **it can't be stressed enough how serious a mistake this is.** Not only will a lack of SO_2 result in a higher frequency of oxidation (acetaldehyde); there is also a higher exposure to microorganisms (i.e., *Lactobacillus*) that have a tendency to give off-character and flavors.

Appendix 5: Equipment List for the Beginning Winemaker

Fermentation, Cellaring, and Storage Gear

Descriptor	Comments
32-gallon food grade container for fermentation	We don't use the term "garbage can."
2 or 3 food grade pails	5-gallon buckets are inexpensive and can be purchased at any hardware store.
2 or 3 carboys and carboy brush	If you plan on making 5 to 10 gallons of wine, have an extra carboy on the side for racking. However, if you plan on making wine in a new or neutral barrel, a few carboys are nice to have for topping wine, and for product lost through racking. Make sure to fill any space between a finished wine and the neck of the carboy with inert gas (i.e., nitrogen, argon) to prevent oxidation. Seal with a nylon plug, or break down and top off into individual gallon jugs.
Carboy funnel	Ideal for filling drums, barrels, tanks, and carboys, providing ample volume and fast flow.

Descriptor	Comments
Rubber stoppers and gas locks for carboys (usually size #6.5 or #7)	Needed during fermentation and malolactic conversion when CO_2 is being released. Once the wine becomes "still" the carboy can be sealed with a solid nylon plug.
Nylon gas release bung and solid nylon bung for barrels	The nylon gas release bung is a barrel plug designed to allow CO_2 gas escape and keep oxygen out. The solid bung is a barrel plug used when the wine becomes still.
Hydrometer	Instrument used to test the level of sugar in must and for measuring potential alcohol.
Racking wand with cap and 6-foot length of $^3/_8$" clear vinyl tubing for siphoning	Used to rack from one carboy to another with gravity feed.
Wine pump (optional)	For productions of 50 gallons or greater (barrel); requires two 6 to 8 foot sections of 5/8" vinyl hose with plastic hose bibs.
Wine thief	Glass or plastic device used to pull wine out of the carboy or barrel. I use a plastic version that I can take apart and put in the dishwasher.

Descriptor	Comments
Inert gases (optional)	For topping barrels or carboys – help prevent oxidation in wine. Both nitrogen and argon can be obtained from your local hardware store or welding supply shop. They are simple to use and non-flammable. You inject the tubing or wand directly in the neck of the carboy or barrel and apply the gas to displace oxygen in the storage container.
Proxyclean, or other sodium percarbonate	Used to clean and sanitize wine equipment and barrels
Trisodium phosphate (TSP)	Used for cleaning heavy grime

Shared or Rented Equipment

Descriptor	Comments
Grape crusher and destemmer	Many times grapes can be purchased from farmers already crushed and a crusher is not necessary. If not, you will need this piece of equipment. This is a good reason to join a club, or rent from your local home winemaking supply shop.
Basket press	This device consists of a fixed plate at the bottom, movable plate at the top, and a cylinder made of wood slats around the sides. The grape *pomace* or pulp is placed in the cylinder; a wooden plate is placed on top and is forced down (pressed) by either a ratcheted threaded screw or hydraulics.
3-Station bottling unit (optional)	You can process single bottles directly from your carboy to the bottle via a siphon hose and nylon shutoff (usually a pincer) connected on the hose. However the 3-station bottler is more convenient for the bigger jobs. Rent, borrow, or buy.
Bottle tree and bottle squirter	Final sanitation of the clean wine bottles, just before bottling. The squirter fits on the top of the bottle tree, is filled with SO_2 solution to sanitize the bottle. The bottle is then placed upside down on the bottle tree to drain.

Descriptor	Comments
Corker and good quality corks	There are many varieties of corkers at various costs depending on the volume of wine you plan to make. Most clubs and all fermentation stores have a corker and quality corks available. Use new sulfated corks to avoid contamination.

Testing Equipment, Chemistry, and Reagents

Descriptor	Comments
500 gm electronic scale	Weighs ingredients to the nearest tenth of a gram – these scales are very cheap online so don't be afraid to explore.
5 lb of potassium metabisulfite (PMBS)	You can never have enough of this chemical. It's used to sanitize equipment, barrels, glass, and of course, in the right dosage, protect your wine from infection and oxidation.
5 lb of citric acid	Enhances the sanitation properties in PMBS during cleaning. Citric acid will neutralize any traces of alkali from other caustic cleaners such as Barrel Kleen or TSP.
5 lb of tartaric acid	Used to increase acid levels (decrease pH) in the must during primary and post-fermentation, if necessary.
1 package freeze-dried ML culture for red wines	Online or available at your local fermentation shop.
Electronic calculator	You will definitely apply your high-school math skills in this profession.
Thermometer	Used for monitoring fermentation progress.

| Electronic pH meter (essential)  | For wine testing and balancing. I recommend the pHep5 pH meter by Hanna Instruments. This instrument runs under $100 and has an *accuracy rate of 0.02 pH with push-button calibration and temperature display.* This instrument combines some of the best features into a very accurate, easy-to-use meter. If the sensor goes bad, it is easily replaced. The meter is less than 8 inches in height. .

Calibrating your pH Meter: - It is important to note that **all digital pH meters need to be calibrated on a regular basis**. Also, as batteries get older, your meter will lose calibration. Calibrate your meter with two pH buffer solutions; pH 7.01 represents a neutral solution, and pH 4.01 represents an acidic solution. These buffers are readily available online or at your local fermentation store. With the pHep5 you simply follow the factory directions (contained in the box) for push-button calibration. It's as simple as that and takes the guesswork out. |

Appendix 6: Documentation – Wine Log

Paper remembers what the mind forgets

I cannot stress enough the importance of documentation. How else will you remember how you made that fantastic wine last year? Unfortunately it's just as important to jot down those "lessons learned" during times when a wine goes bad, so those mistakes are not repeated.

The wine log example provided in this appendix records harvest details, chemistry makeup during primary fermentation, racking, post-fermentation lab analysis, and other adjustments. The Wine Log is designed to assist you in creating the best product possible.

Wine Log - Page 1

Date Picked _____

Lot number or name _____

Vineyard name and location _____

Varietal(s) by percentage _____   Weight _____ #'s   Potential Alcohol _____ %

Initial Sugar: Brix _____ B°   Final Adjusted Sugar: Brix _____ B°   Water Added _____ gal/ltrs

Primary Fermentation:

Date	Description or Action Taken	Brix (B°)	Temp (°F)	Additional Detail
			°F	

Pre-Post Fermentation:

Date	Racking/Lab Analysis/Other Adjustments	pH	Acid	Free SO₂	Additional Detail or Actions Taken

Date Bottled: _____

Wine Log Sample - Completed

Winemaking Log for Stone Step Cellars - Page 1
Date Picked 09/10/10
Lot number or name Zinfandel - Lot 1
Aparicio Vineyards - Sutter Creek California

Varietal(s) by percentage	(i.e. 25% Zin, 75% Cabernet)	Weight	1000 #'s	Potential Alcohol	13.50%
Initial Sugar:	(Brix) 28.5 B°	Final Adjusted Sugar:	24.5 B°	Water Added	12 gals

Primary Fermentation:

Date	Description or Action Taken	Brix (B°)	Temp. (°F)	Additional Detail
9/10/2010	Added 12 gallons water	28.5 B°	65°F	Ameriolate with water to bring sugars down
9/11/2010	Add Superfood and yeast	24.5 B°	65°F	Add 1/3 of Superfood to begin fermentation
9/12/2010	Fermentation begins	24.5 B°	70°F	Punching scheduled for AM, Noon and PM
9/13/2010	Fermentation in full bloom	22.5 B°	80°F	
9/14/2010	Add second dose of Superfood	14.5 B°	85°F	Add 1/3 of Superfood in middle of fermentation
9/15/2010 AM	Healthy ferment	7.5 B°	86°F	Temperature peaked
9/15/2010 PM	Add last dose of Superfood	4.0 B°	78°F	Plan to press on 9/17/10
9/16/2010	Add ML Bacterium	1.5 B°	75°F	Added 1 pkg of freeze dried ML Bacterium
9/17/2010	Pressed	0.5 B°	70°F	Pressed into 1 barrel and 3 carboys

Pre-Post Fermentation:

Date	Racking/Lab Analysis/Other Adjustments	pH	Acid	Free SO₂	Additional Detail or Actions Taken
9/11/2010	Tested pH, Acid	3.85	0.35	0	Add 14 oz tartaric acid
10/17/2010	First racking	3.7	0.5	0	First rack - ML still active
11/2/2010	ML testing	3.65	0.55	0	ML completed, added 40 ppm SO₂
11/30/2010	Tested pH, Acid	3.65	0.55	20ppm	Added 3.9 oz tartaric acid
2/20/2011	2nd racking	3.55	0.6	15ppm	Added 25 ppm SO₂
5/30/2011	3rd racking, tested pH and acid	3.6	0.59	25 ppm	Added 15 ppm SO₂ and 2 oz tartaric acid
8/10/2011	Test and adjust SO₂	3.55		40 ppm	Added 10 ppm SO₂ prior to filtering and Bottling

Date Bottled: 8/12/2011

Appendix 7: Conversion Tables

The tables below can be useful when converting between US and metric measures:

Volume Conversion

1 US tablespoon	=	3 US teaspoons
1 US fluid ounce (fl oz)	=	29.5735 milliliters (mL)
1 US cup	=	16 US tablespoons
1 US cup	=	8 US fluid ounces (fl oz)
1 US cup	=	0.2365 liters (l)
1 US pint	=	2 US cups
1 US pint	=	16 US fluid ounces (fl oz)
1 US pint	=	0.4731 liters (l)
1 liter (l)	=	1,000 milliliters (mL)
1 US quart	=	2 US pints
1 US quart	=	16 US fluid ounces (fl oz)
1 US quart	=	0.9462 liters (l)
1 US gallon	=	4 US quarts
1 US gallon	=	3.7854 liters (l)

Conversion Tables

Weight Conversion

1 milligram (mg)	=	0.001 grams (g)
1 gram (g)	=	0.001 kilograms (kg)
1 gram (g)	=	0.035273962 ounces (oz)
1 ounce (oz)	=	28.34952312 grams (g)
1 ounce (oz)	=	0.0625 pounds (lb)
1 pound (lb)	=	16 ounces (oz)
1 pound (lb)	=	0.45359237 kilograms (kg)
1 kilogram (kg)	=	1,000 grams (g)
1 kilogram (kg)	=	35.273962 ounces (oz)
1 kilogram (kg)	=	2.20462262 pounds (lb)
1 stone	=	14 pounds (lb)
1 short ton	=	2000 pounds (lb)
1 metric ton	=	1,000 kilograms (kg)

Glossary

Glossary of Winemaking Terms

A

Aging – storing wine in barrels, carboys, or bottles for a period of months before consumption. The aging process allows a wine to mellow and properly develop its distinct character.

Acid – one of the three essential structural components of wine. The level of acid determines the freshness, dullness, tartness, and shelf time. Grapes contain many types of acids with tartaric, malic, and citric in dominance. The proper acid level is critical for a healthy fermentation of the must.

Alcohol – during fermentation, yeast eats natural sugars in the must and creates two components in equal amounts: alcohol and carbon dioxide (CO_2). Higher sugar content = higher alcohol content.

B

Blending – the mixing of two or more wines, either the same or different varietals, for purposes of enhancing or correcting the character of your finished product. For example, Bordeaux is a blend of Cabernet Sauvignon, Cabernet Franc, and Merlot or other varietal from the Bordeaux appellation.

Bioflavonoids – antioxidants found in wine that help eliminate free radicals in the body by inhibiting the oxidation of other molecules, thus reducing the risk of heart disease, stroke, asthma, inflammation, and other health related diseases caused by these free radicals.

Brettanomyces – also known as Brett, is a fungal infection originating from the vineyard or contaminated wine equipment, facility, or barrels. Characteristics associated with Brett include a barnyard, musty, or leathery aroma. Good cellaring and SO_2 practices are essential in combating the growth of Brett.

C

Calcium carbonate – an element in winemaking used to reduce the levels of acid in wine (deacidification).

Cap – a solid mass of grape skins, bugs, stems, and seeds that float to the top of the grape must during fermentation. As the CO_2 gas is captured under the cap, it pushes the mass to the top.

Carbon dioxide (CO_2) – a gas produced through fermentation. CO_2 is also an inert gas used to top off tanks or to move a wine when racking. CO_2 is more commonly known as the bubbles in soft drinks.

Carboy – large glass or plastic container similar to that used to hold bottled water. Carboys usually range in sizes of 3, 5, or 6½ gallons and are used in all aspects of wine making, including fermentation, racking, and storing.

Cold soaking – extended submersion of fruit, skins, stems, and seeds in a nonalcoholic setting in which the extraction process is used to improve red wine color and to provide color stability. Cold soaking is sometimes practiced commercially, with the appropriate facility and equipment, to lessen the risk of oxidation. However, this process is optional and should not be attempted by the beginning winemaker.

Cold stabilization – As wines begin to clarify, leftover tartrate salts (tartaric acid) appear in the wine (more prominently in whites). These crystals do not affect the taste; however, they may be considered a flaw. Cold stabilization is the method of chilling a wine at or below freezing to form tartaric crystals on the bottom and sides of the holding container, allowing the winemaker to rack the wine off these crystals.

E

Enology – science of winemaking.

Extended maceration – process of soaking a grape must after primary fermentation and before pressing. The increase in soak time allows the normally short-chained tannin molecules to form longer chains, in effect integrating the tannins into the wine, giving it a softer richer mouth feel; similar to bottle aging. Not recommended for the beginning winemaker unless you have the facilities to control oxidation, volatile acidity (VA) buildup, or bacterial development.

F

Filtering – method of clarifying wine by using a wine pump and filter to eliminate leftover yeast cells and other impurities. For red wine, filtering is performed prior to or on bottling day for a final brilliant product.

Fining – process of cleaning haze or protein matter from a wine using chemical or natural substances (fining agents). The fining agent is stirred into the wine and allowed to settle. Types of fining agents include bentonite, Sparkolloid, even egg whites.

Free-run wine – fermented juice that is pumped or bucketed directly from the fermentation tank without pressing; usually contains lower pH and tannins than the pressed juice.

H

Hydrogen sulfide (H_2S) – a gas produced by yeast having a "permanent solution" or "'rotten egg" aroma. Many times, the problem of hydrogen sulfide can be remedied by splashing the wine during racking, forcing the gas to release in the air. This, followed up with a dose of SO_2 (after ML), will usually do the trick. However, in stubborn cases, copper sulfate is often used to remove H_2S.

L

Lactic acid – an acid found in wine in small amounts. However, during malolactic fermentation, the harsher malic acids are converted to the softer lactic acids (also found in milk) to contribute to an overall smoother mouth feel. Chardonnays that have gone through ML transformation are considered to have "buttery" qualities.

Lees – sediment in wine consisting of dead yeast cells and other particles (bug parts)

M

Malolactic (ML) fermentation (also known as secondary fermentation) – the process of converting malolactic (sharp) acid to lactic (soft) acid, giving it a smoother flavor. Malolactic fermentation is achieved by inoculating the wine with lactic acid bacteria. A Chardonnay that has gone through malolactic fermentation is usually considered to have "buttery" characteristics.

Must – original crushed grapes prior to and during fermentation and extended maceration; includes the grape stems, seeds, skins, and juice that are used to create wine.

O

Oxidation – usually in the form of acetaldehyde; occurs from the exposure of developing wine with oxygen. Oxidation will cause browning and off characteristics and is considered a fault in wine. To prevent oxidation, promote good cellar practices by topping off aging and storage containers and maintaining appropriate levels of SO_2 in the wine.

P

Pectic enzyme – used during fermentation, helps to extract colors, break down pulp, and clear protein hazes. This is an optional treatment in winemaking.

Pitching – adding yeast or other component to the grape must.

Pomace – after pressing, the grape material left behind. Pomace breaks down quickly in the compost pile or worm bin, ready to be reused in your garden and landscaping.

Primary fermentation – the process of turning grapes into wine. During primary fermentation yeast begins to eat the natural sugars in the must to form alcohol and carbon dioxide. Primary fermentation is complete once all the sugar is consumed or the cultured yeast dies, whichever comes first. If the latter occurs, a wine is considered to have *residual sugar*.

R

Racking – the process of clarifying wine by siphoning wine off the grape lees into a new container, leaving the sediment behind.

Residual sugar – the amount of sweetness left in the wine associated with unfermented sugars. Residual sugar usually occurs during stuck fermentation, or when alcohol exceeds the alcohol tolerance of a specific yeast strain, or through the use of potassium sorbate and/or high-proof alcohol.

S

Sulfite – usually in the form of potassium metabisulfite, a component added to wine to inhibit the growth of wild yeast, bind with acetaldehyde, and keep certain bacteria in check. Sulfites are also used for cleaning and sanitizing equipment and storage containers. The use of sulfites is essential in winemaking.

Sur lie (French) – the process where the wine is allowed to sit on its *fine lees* for quite some time before being racked off. For many Chardonnays, the lees are occasionally stirred into the wine during this time to gain aroma, flavor, and richness. However, wine allowed to sit on its *gross lees* for long periods can end up having hydrogen sulfide issues. This process is definitely optional.

T

Tannins – derived from the grape skins, stems, and seeds and are alcohol soluble. Tannins are an important element for aging; they are normally rough, astringent compounds capable in high levels to pucker the senses. Tannins are also derived from oak products that can increase the complexity and shelf life of the wine. Over time through polymerization tannin molecular chains will link up and precipitate out (in the form of sediment) and eventually soften. Tannins also contain abundant and powerful antioxidant properties.

Topping off – the process of filling the empty air space in a barrel or other wine container (with wine or inert gas) to reduce the risk of oxidation.

V

Vintage – the year the grapes were harvested.

Volatile acidity, or VA – usually derived from excessive levels of acetic acid bacteria that early on can give off aromas like those of acetone or nail polish remover. If left unchecked, VA can produce vinegary characteristics in nose and taste, or result in the conversion of alcohol to ethyl acetate in solvent-like qualities. VA requires oxygen to grow; this is one more reason to maintain good cellaring practices by topping off and frequently checking the SO_2 levels.

Glossary of Tasting Terms

A

Aftertaste – also associated with the "finish" and "length"; the flavor or sensation of the wine in the mouth after swallowing. The length of the finish or aftertaste is also a determination of the quality and complexity of the wine.

Acidity – the mutual effect between fruit (sweetness) and acid (tartness) is usually referred to as the balance or structure of a wine. High acid levels are usually detected as sharp, tart sensations to the mouth, which often can be desirable in white wine but not always in red. Conversely, the absence of good acidity can make wine dull and flabby.

Alcohol (or "proof") – This element contributes to the finish, balance, and structure of the wine. A wine with balanced alcohol levels can enhance its overall mouth feel and texture. A wine with too little alcohol can give off weak or watery characters, whereas a wine too high in alcohol could be considered "hot."

B

Backward – a wine that is considered not ready for prime time or one that needs a little more shelf time. Most are newer wines with high tannins, needing some time to smooth out and meld the flavors.

Balance – A wine is considered *balanced* when the sugars, acid, flavor, and tannins have a positive mutual effect to each other, becoming harmonious in nature.

Blind tasting – a method used in competitions and sometimes in social circles for purposes of judging wine without influencing the taster. In blending, the percentage of varietal blends is hidden from the taster so as not to influence the decision.

Body (or weight) – When you say a wine is thin, buttery, watery, or creamy, you are describing the wine's body. Essentially it is the perceived texture of the solution. Of the five senses, you could possibly categorize this under touch or mouth feel.

C

Closed – A wine that is not quite ready for prime time is tight in nature and its components (such as sugars, acid, and tannins) are not in harmony, is considered closed. It is usually a young wine not meeting its potential, having no distinct aroma and very little complexity. The remedy: more shelf time.

Color – Pigment is derived from the grape skins and is water soluble, whereas tannins are alcohol soluble. White wine comes from white grapes, red wine from red grapes, and rosés from red wines, which are pressed off the skins prior to fermentation and before significant colors can leach off. The color can describe a lot about wine, whether it's young (intense and vibrant), old (muted), or oxidized (tawny).

Corked (trichloroanisole, or TCA) – A wine is said to be corked when it is contaminated by a chemical compound (mold infection) found in cork stoppers. A corked wine is described as having a musty or "old barrel" aroma. Flavor and texture are also adversely affected. A corked wine should always be returned when served at a restaurant.

D

Dry – having no perceived sweetness.

F

Finish – the flavor or sensation of the wine in the mouth after swallowing (also refer to *aftertaste*).

H

Hollow – used to describe a wine with no redeeming values, perhaps lacking texture, flavor, or depth.

I

Integrated – A wine is considered *integrated* when sugars, acid, oak, and other components fade and become harmonious as the wine develops (also see *balance*).

L

Legs – Visually, legs appear as tears running back into a wine after swirling. Legs do not directly relate to the quality of wine, merely the level of alcohol contained in the wine and the surface tension associated with alcohol.

Length – The length of the finish or aftertaste is a determination of the quality and complexity of the wine. Length is the amount of time a wine will persist on the tongue or palate after it is swallowed or spit out (during judging).

M

Madeirisation – A wine that is oxidized giving a port or sherry-like aroma has gone through madeirisation. This is usually a fault and occurs mostly in white wines; however, it is an acceptable characteristic for late-harvest and some dessert wine, such as Madeira. Madeirisation is often the result of poor storage or cellaring. Keep the tanks topped off and watch the SO_2 levels.

Mid-palate – The mid-palate or "middle range phase" is the judging factor for flavor, texture, acidity, and tannins of the wine. The mid-palate is the actual taste of the wine. This sensory factor along with the nose allows the taster to discern the primary berry, oaky, spicy, earthy flavors and other secondary flavor characteristics of a wine.

N

Nose – wine aroma or bouquet. Once a wine is on the mid-palate, the nose is the determining factor for the perceived flavor in the mouth. During judging, the nose is the critical factor for identifying varietal characteristics and detecting wine flaws (i.e., corked wine, Brett, etc.). During fermentation and cellaring, it is the nose that alerts the winemaker to potential issues such as hydrogen sulfide and acetaldehyde. When in doubt, follow the nose.

S

Five S's – the five steps wine drinkers employ when enjoying their craft:
- Swirl – oxygenate the wine to release the bouquet
- Sniff – smell and enjoy the bouquet and aroma
- Sip – taste the fruit and flavor components
- Savor – allow the wine to linger on the tongue and feel the structure
- Swallow – enjoy

Five Senses – all senses are used when wine tasting:
- Taste – perceived flavors of the wine
- Touch – texture or body of the wine in the mouth
- Smell – aroma or bouquet of the wine
- Hearing – effervescence related to fermentation or sparkling wine
- Sight – color and clarity of the wine

Structure – When you think of structure, you think of the way something is built. Likewise, wine structure is the elements of construction in a wine, including the acid, tannins, and alcohol that give the wine its perceived flavor and texture. There are three types of structure to consider: 1) weak structured – considered as watery, flat, or flabby; 2) strong structured – considered harsh, acidic, or tannic; and 3) well structured – considered balanced and complex. Wines that age well are those that have high structure in the beginning but later become well structured.

T

Tannic – Tannins are derived from the stems, seeds, and peels of the grape; they are astringent in nature, causing a dry, puckery feeling in the mouth. The dryness and astringency will begin to precipitate out and mellow as the wine ages. A wine with high tannic properties will have a longer shelf life and gain good structure as it ages.

Toasty – In almost all cases, a wine with "toasty" characteristics is one aged in an oak barrel or other oak product (oak spirals, spheres, staves, etc.). Most oak products come in a variety of "toast" factors, including: 1) light toast – used in some white wines; 2) medium toast – light body reds (Pinots, Sangiovese) or heavier whites (Chardonnay); 3) heavy toast – medium to heavy bodied wines (Zinfandels); and 4) and heavy plus toast – big or full-bodied reds (Petite Syrah). One must be careful not to over-oak; that could overwhelm the varietal characteristics of the fruit. Therefore, sniff, swirl, and sip often to ensure the optimum flavor and structure of the wine.

Simple Tasting Descriptors

Visual

Visual descriptor	Definition
Bright or brilliant	A clear appearance without haziness or floating particles
Clear	Transparent
Dark	Opposed to light in color
Garnet/Ruby	Red in color, medium in shade
Straw	Pale shade of yellow
Opaque	Dark in color, lacking transparency

Aroma

Aromatic descriptor	Definition
Bouquet	Wine's aroma
Complex	Harmonious aromas
Dark fruits	A complex aroma of fruits such as blackberries, Marion berries, and Santa Rosa plums
Earth	Peat or forest floor
Jammy	Ripe berry
Nose	The aroma itself, or its description
Pepper	Spicy, black, or white peppered
Red fruits	Complex aroma of fruits such as raspberries, cherries, and red plums
Simple	Lacking complexity

Aromatic descriptor continuted	Definition
Smoky	Charred oak
Spicy	Anise, cloves

Flavors

Flavor descriptor	Definition
Attack	Initial flavors tasted
Acid	Tart or sour
Balance	Harmonious flavors
Bitter	Sharp or disagreeable
Body	Weight or fullness in the mouth
Bright	Fresh sensation
Brooding	Weighty but undefined flavors
Buttery	Tastes like butter
Chewy	Puckery sensation with substantial tannins
Clean	Flawless
Crisp	Bright flavors with acidic balance
Complex	Layers of flavor
Dry	An absence of sweetness
Flat	Lacking flavor or no longer bubbly
Forward	Noticeable fruit flavors
Full-bodied	A mouth-filling sensation
Jammy	Tastes of ripe berries

Flavor descriptor continued	Definition
Medium-bodied	A moderate degree of fullness in the mouth
Racy	Bright tasting with acidic balance
Residual sugar	Sweetness from unfermented sugar
Robust	Hearty and mouth-filling
Smooth	Balanced with tannin, acid, and fruit
Tannins	Grape seeds, stems, and oak barrels responsible for a red wine's puckery sensation
Velvety	A gentle, supple texture
Youthful	Bright, exuberant, and fruit forward

Common Wine Defects

A

Acetaldehyde – Originates during pre-fermentation or fermentation phases due to microbial changes or contamination but also can develop during bulk aging. Sensory detection of acetaldehyde occurs during bulk aging, having characteristics similar to late harvest wine or sherry. Causes of acetaldehyde during post-fermentation could occur from ethanol oxidation or the occurrence of surface film from inadequate cellar.

Correction or Prevention: During fermentation, stabilize must with SO_2 after harvest, add appropriate cultured yeasts, provide adequate levels of nutrition, avoid excessive exposure to oxygen especially during extended maceration, exercise good cellar hygiene, and avoid cross-contamination of equipment.

Post-fermentation prevention techniques include maintaining SO_2 levels at appropriate molecular levels (SO_2 binds to acetaldehyde) and limiting oxygen exposure to the finished wine during bulk aging by topping storage containers.

Acetic acid (a.k.a. volatile acid, or VA) – Usually originates during pre-fermentation and fermentation caused from wine spoilage bacteria and/or yeasts. However, VA can occur during bulk aging through improper cellar practices (i.e., improperly filled containers). Acetic acid can be detected through sensory evaluation, giving wine a vinegary or sour taste.

Correction or Prevention: During fermentation, stabilize must with SO_2 after harvest, add appropriate cultured yeasts, provide adequate levels of nutrition, avoid excessive exposure to oxygen, exercise good cellar hygiene, and avoid cross-contamination.

Post-fermentation prevention techniques include maintaining SO_2 levels at appropriate molecular levels and topping wine storage containers.

B

Brettanomyces (a.k.a. Brett) – Considered a wine spoilage yeast and often originates in barrels or contaminated cellars during bulk aging. Many commercial wineries contain these spoilage yeasts within their facilities but maintain good sanitation practices to control the problem. Brett is particularly attracted to cellulose in new oak barrels. Brett is detected through sensory evaluation having both pleasant (spice and cloves) and not so pleasant (barnyard, leather, Novocain, Band-Aid) aromas.

At low levels Brett can be considered desirable with respect to wine complexity and interest. However,

Brett is almost always considered a fault by individuals who have a low sensory tolerance to this spoilage yeast.

Correction or Prevention: If low levels of Brett are detected it is important to squelch further growth by maintaining adequate SO_2 levels at appropriate molecular levels. Other preventive controls include SO_2 stabilization after harvest, inoculation with a known cultured yeast strain, providing adequate levels of nutrition, covering the primary fermentation container to limit insect and air contamination, exercising good sanitation and barrel maintenance practices, and avoiding cross-contamination of equipment.

C

Cork taint or Trichloroanisole (TCA) – Usually occurs during bulk aging from exposure to bacteria or molds in wood, and oftentimes through contact with chlorinated surfaces, contaminated corks, or chlorinated water. TCA can be detected through sensory evaluation as having earthy, wet paper, or moldy wet basement aromas that cover up the fruity characteristics in wine.

Correction or Prevention: To control, always use new sulfated corks when bottling and avoid chlorine based cleaning products; use non-odorized products such as Trisodium Phosphate (TSP), ProxyClean, or Barrel Kleen, followed up with an SO_2/citric acid rinse.

D

Diacetyl – Originates during fermentation as a by-product of lactic acid bacteria; usually occurs after malolactic fermentation in which residual ML bacteria may remain in the wine and metabolize. Diacetyl is often strived for in creating buttery sensations in a white wine, especially Chardonnays, and softening red wines. However, if remaining levels of ML bacteria are allowed to metabolize, diacetyl can take on characteristics similar to rancid butter.

Correction or Prevention: Keep wine on stirred lees until undesirable characteristics have dissipated, or carefully rack the wine off remaining lees after ML fermentation and maintain adequate SO_2 levels.

E

Ethyl acetate – Usually occurs during pre-fermentation or fermentation phases. Ethyl acetate can be detected through sensory evaluation as having solvent-like characteristics similar to nail polish remover or acetone. This defect is usually caused from wild yeast ferments and/or bacterial development.

Correction or Prevention: During fermentation, stabilize must with SO_2 after harvest, add appropriate cultured yeasts, provide adequate levels of nutrition, avoid excessive oxidation especially during extended maceration, exercise good cellar hygiene, and avoid cross-contamination of wine making equipment.

Post-fermentation techniques include maintaining SO_2 levels at appropriate molecular levels and limiting oxygen exposure by topping off containers.

H

Hydrogen sulfide (H_2S) – Usually originates during fermentation as a by-product of yeast fermentation in a must containing limited nitrogen. Hydrogen sulfide (a.k.a. volatile sulfur compounds) can be detected through sensory evaluation as having rotten egg or sulfur characteristics.

Correction or Prevention: Stabilize must with SO_2 after harvest, inoculate with a known cultured yeast strain, add nutrient and nitrogen supplements such as diammonium phosphate (DAP) or Superfood, control oxidation of must, and reduce time spent on gross lees after fermentation.

M

Mercaptin (a.k.a. ethanethiol) – Usually originates during fermentation as a reaction to hydrogen sulfide, especially if the wine is allowed to sit on its gross lees for an extended period. Mercaptin (another volatile sulfur compound) can be detected through sensory evaluation as having slight onion, rubber, or natural gas-like aromas.

Correction or Prevention: Stabilize must with SO_2 after harvest, inoculate with a known cultured yeast strain, add nutrient and nitrogen supplements, control oxidation of must, and reduce the time spent on gross lees after fermentation.

S

Sulfur dioxide (SO$_2$) – Usually occurs during bulk aging from over-sulfating the wine. Sulfur dioxide can be detected through sensory evaluation as having characteristics similar to a burnt match or sulfur stick.

Completely preventable by maintaining adequate SO$_2$ levels at appropriate molecular levels, being careful not to over-dose.

INDEX

measuring and
adjustment of,
21–24
Sulfur dioxide
applicaiton of, 81
wine fault, 128
Tannins
bulk aging, 41
effect of extended
maceration, 32
extraction of, 14
Tartaric acid, 24, 25,
55
Tartaric crystals, 55
Temperature
documentation of,
12
improper storage of,
60
Terroir, 5

The crush, 8
Topping off during
bulk aging, 41
Total SO_2, 45, 49
Trichloroanisole
TCA, 125
Varietals, 5
Volatile sulfur
compounds, 127
Where to find grapes,
7
Winemakers club, 9
Winemaking
equipment, 87–93
Yeasts
customizing your
wines, 29
defn of, 11
rehydration, 29

Resources

Wine Labs, Fermentation Catalogs, and Product Specifications

Lallemand North America – www.lallemandwine.us
- Tel: 707-526-9809
- Fermentation supplies and product specification
- Fermentation supply catalog upon request

Scott Laboratories – www.scottlab.com
- Tel: 707-765-6666; and Pickering, ON – Tel: 905-839-9463
- Fermentation supplies and product specification
- Fermentation supply catalog upon request

Vinquiry – www.vinquiry.com
- Winsor, CA – Tel: 707-838-6312; Napa, CA – Tel: 707-259-0740; and Santa Maria, CA – Tel: 805-922-6321
- Wine lab services and education
- Wine chemistry and glassware

Gusmer Enterprises – www.gusmerenterprises.com
- Fresno, CA - Tel: 559-485-2692; Mountainside, NJ – Tel: 908-301-1811; Napa, CA – Tel: 707-224-7903; and Waupaca, WI - Tel: 715-258-5525
- Wine lab services
- Wine chemistry and glassware
- Fermentation supplies and product specifications

- Fermentation supply catalog upon request

Lodi Wine Lab – www.lodiwinerylaboratory.com
- Lodi, Ca – Tel: 209-339-1990
- Wine lab services
- Wine chemistry and glassware
- Fermentation supplies and product specifications.

Wyeast Laboratories – www.wyeastlab.com
- Fermentation supplies and product specification

ETS Laboratories – www.etslabs.com
- Various locations throughout the West Coast
- Wine lab services

Fermentis, a division of Lesaffre Group – www.fermentis.com
- Red Star yeast and product specification

White Labs – www.whitelabs.com
- White Star yeast products and ML bacteria cultures
- Online product specification

Notes

Notes

Notes

Notes

Made in the USA
Lexington, KY
19 September 2011